Building Character, Community, and a Growth Mindset in Physical Education

Activities That Promote Learning and Emotional and Social Development

Leigh Anderson, MA
Donald R. Glover, MA

HUMAN KINETICS

Library of Congress Cataloging-in-Publication Data

Names: Anderson, Leigh Ann, 1969- author. | Glover, Donald R., author.
Title: Building character, community, and a growth mindset in physical
  education : activities that promote learning and emotional and social
  development / Leigh Anderson, MA, Donald R. Glover, MA.
Description: Champaign, IL : Human Kinetics, [2017]
Identifiers: LCCN 2016031662| ISBN 9781492536680 (print) | ISBN 9781492548232
  (ebook)
Subjects: LCSH: Physical education for children--Study and teaching--Activity
  programs. | Moral education (Elementary) | Social learning.
Classification: LCC GV443 .A468 2017 | DDC 372.86--dc23 LC record available at https://lccn.loc.
  gov/2016031662

ISBN: 978-1-4925-3668-0 (print)

Paul Shirilla, PhD, department chairman, and outdoor education professor at the University of Wisconsin at River Falls, incorporated several popular outdoor activities into team-building challenges featured in chapter 5. Great ideas for that chapter were also provided by Victoria A. Otto, who was 2011 Secondary PE Teacher of the Year for the Illinois Association for Health, Physical Education, Recreation and Dance and 2012 Secondary PE Teacher of the Year for the SHAPE Midwest district.

The web addresses cited in this text were current as of October 2016, unless otherwise noted.

Acquisitions Editor: Scott Wikgren; **Senior Developmental Editor:** Bethany J. Bentley; **Managing Editors:** B. Rego, Anne Cole, and Anna Lan Seaman; **Copyeditor:** Tom Tiller; **Permissions Manager:** Dalene Reeder; **Graphic Designers:** Kathleen Boudreau-Fuoss and Whitney Milburn; **Cover Designer:** Keith Blomberg; **Photograph (cover):** Christopher Futcher/Getty Images; **Senior Art Manager:** Kelly Hendren; **Illustrations:** © Human Kinetics, unless otherwise noted; **Printer:** Versa Press

Printed in the United States of America   10 9 8 7 6 5 4

The paper in this book is certified under a sustainable forestry program.

Human Kinetics
1607 N. Market Street
Champaign, IL 61820
USA

United States and International
Website: **US.HumanKinetics.com**
Email: info@hkusa.com
Phone: 1-800-747-4457

Canada
Website: **Canada.HumanKinetics.com**
Email: info@hkcanada.com

Tell us what you think!
Human Kinetics would love to hear what we
can do to improve the customer experience.
Use this QR code to take our brief survey.

E6902

This book is dedicated to my mom, Carol, and dad, Don.

Mom, thanks for always making your kids and grandkids
feel like they are the most important and loved people on earth.

Dad, there is no one who motivates and inspires others more than you.
You have a unique ability to bring out the best in others
through your compassion, enthusiasm, knowledge, and humor.

I love you both, and I couldn't be more proud to be your daughter.

— *Leigh Anderson*

I would like to dedicate this book to Cora, William,
Sammy, Ruthie, and Nora.

These grandchildren and great grandchildren are keeping us young.

— *Don Glover*

Contents

Activity Finder

Preface

Physical education and sport provide the perfect environment to teach valuable life skills and core values, help students prepare for college and career, and help them become personally and socially responsible. Therefore, as a coach or physical educator, you hold the power to inspire and elicit positive change in your students—in terms of not only their health but also their personal and professional lives. This influence enhances the value of the role you play at your school; indeed, it is vital to the school's overall mission. However, physical education and sport can also provide an environment conducive to bullying. The antidote to bullying is to teach students to be respectful competitors, supportive teammates, and successful citizens.

The value of these benefits—cognitive, emotional, and social development; college and career readiness; personal and social responsibility; and bullying prevention—are now widely recognized by educators and potential employers. Here are a few examples:

- Society of Health and Physical Educators' (SHAPE America) National Standards and Grade-Level Outcomes for K-12 Physical Education states that a "physically literate individual exhibits responsible personal and social behavior that respects self and others" (standard 4) and "recognizes the value of physical activity for health, enjoyment, challenge, self-expression, and/or social interaction" (standard 5).

- Also in the United States, the sixth standard put forth by the National Board for Professional Teaching Standards (NBPTS) states that accomplished teachers of physical education create and sustain welcoming, safe, and challenging environments in which students engage in and enjoy physical activity. These teachers establish an orderly atmosphere with established protocols and expectations that facilitate maximum learning for all students. Learning is enhanced when students learn in a community and feel connected to those around them.

- Physical and Health Education Canada (PHE Canada) states that physical education should promote key character traits, such as fair play, cooperation, and teamwork, through physical activities. It also states that all physical activities should be infused with opportunities to develop life skills, including cooperation, positive communication, leadership, personal and social management, decision making, problem solving, conflict resolution, stress management, interpersonal skills, and spiritual and moral development.

- Fortune 500 companies list teamwork, problem solving, and interpersonal skills as the three most important skills for employees.

In *Building Character, Community, and a Growth Mindset in Physical Education*, we provide you with a road map and ready-to-use activities to help your students achieve SHAPE America's standards 4 and 5; to help you achieve NBPTS standard 6 and PHE Canada's goals for physical education; and to prepare your students to succeed in college, in the workplace, and in their personal lives. In the process, you will also enhance your value to your school and your community.

Here is a brief look at the specific content of the book's chapters, as well as the web resource. Chapter 1 explores the connection between emotional intelligence and a growth mindset. It reinforces the many ways in which physical education and sport are the ideal settings to build college and career-readiness skills. Chapter 2 describes the impact community building has on motivation and learning. Students are more successful when they feel connected and supported by those around them. This chapter provides activities for strengthening relationships in ways that are fun, active, and motivational. It emphasizes the importance of empowering students to take an active role in their learning.

Chapter 3 includes strategies for building character in every lesson delivered. Through physical education and sport, you can help young people learn how to be supportive teammates and respectful competitors, how to solve problems, and how to overcome adversity. These character traits are necessary in order to succeed on the field, on the rink, in the classroom, in the workplace, and in personal relationships. To help you implement these strategies, chapter 4 presents 20 character-building activities. These creative activities provide a unique way to integrate exercise through community and character-building games.

Chapter 5 introduces how emotional intelligence and a growth mindset can be strengthened through team building. It provides 11 team-building challenges. Chapter 6 then delves deeper into a growth mindset and makes direct connections to reflection, assessment, and goal setting.

The book's web resource provides you with editable and printable versions of activity materials, including focus words, challenge cards, worksheets, and much more. For quick reference, thumbnail-sized versions of these materials are placed throughout the book itself. To access the web resource, visit www.Human Kinetics.com/BuildingCharacterCommunityAndA GrowthMindsetInPhysicalEducation.

eBook

available at
HumanKinetics.com

Teaching youth to be resilient kids of character while facilitating a love for fitness is the central focus of this book. The two concepts are naturally integrated through many engaging, meaningful, and challenging activities. Maximizing the potential of students and athletes is the hope and dream of every teacher and coach. Reaching one's full potential, however, requires sacrifice, perseverance, and hard work. The activities and lesson plans presented in this book focus on the process of growth and the skills needed to overcome adversity, work in collaboration, and set and reach goals. Embracing a growth mindset and learning how to maintain active, healthy lifestyles will set youth up for success socially, emotionally, and physically long after their experiences in school and sports. We learn not for school but for life.

How to Access the Web Resource

Throughout *Building Character, Community, and a Growth Mindset in Physical Education*, you will find previews of activity materials that can be found in the web resource. This online content is available to you free of charge when you purchase a new print or electronic version of the book. The web resource offers printable activity materials, such as focus words, challenge cards, handouts, and more. To access the online content, simply register with the Human Kinetics website. Here's how:

1. Visit www.HumanKinetics.com/BuildingCharacterCommunityAndAGrowth MindsetInPhysicalEducation.

2. Click the First Edition link next to the corresponding first-edition book cover.

3. Click the Sign In link on the left or at the top of the page. If you do not have an account with Human Kinetics, you will be prompted to create one.

4. Once you have registered, if the online product does not appear in the Ancillary Items box at the left, click the Enter Pass Code option in that box. Enter the following pass code exactly as it is printed here, including any capitalization and hyphens: **ANDERSON-3KH2R-WR**

5. Click the Submit button to unlock your online product.

6. After you have entered your pass code for the first time, you will never have to enter it again in order to access this online product. Once you have unlocked your product, a link to the product will appear permanently in the menu on the left. All you need to do to access your online content on subsequent visits is sign in to www.HumanKinetics.com/BuildingCharacterCommunityAndAGrowthMindsetInPhysicalEducation and follow the link!

If you need assistance along the way, click the Need Help? button on the book's website.

Strengthening Emotional Intelligence

I've missed more than 9,000 shots in my career.
I've lost almost 300 games. Twenty-six times I've been
trusted to take the game-winning shot and missed.
I've failed over and over and over again in my life.
And that is why I succeed.

Michael Jordan, NBA basketball legend

Emotional intelligence involves being aware of our emotions and how we react to them. Consider how often students quit or get angry when they experience failure or frustration. Now imagine what it would be like if those students developed a growth mindset in which they expected and embraced frustrating emotions and recognized how those emotions can contribute to their growth and improvement. We need to teach and reinforce habits for overcoming adversity, both individually and collaboratively, just as much as we teach reading, writing, and math.

There is no better environment for nurturing emotional skills in students than physical education and sport. Themes such as teamwork, competition, goal setting, problem solving, and perseverance are natural ingredients in athletics and physical fitness, and they also form the pillars of success in life. All too often, however, physical education and sport activities focus only on the relevant physical capacities and sport-specific skills. If we are intentional about connecting these physical components of athletics to the emotional components, we give students a much greater chance of enjoying healthy, active lives.

In this chapter, you will learn to

- define emotional intelligence,
- foster understanding among students,
- facilitate strategies for success, and
- prepare students for both college and career.

DEFINING EMOTIONAL INTELLIGENCE

Optimism, flexibility, ability to defuse conflict, impulse control, self-motivation, overcoming adversity—these are a few of the many traits (often referred to as "soft skills") that make up emotional intelligence. One way to consider emotional intelligence is through the concept of emotional quotient (EQ), which addresses how well a person handles his or her own emotions, as well as the emotions of others. Of course, the more familiar concept of intelligence quotient (IQ) is used in attempts to quantify a person's ability to learn, understand, and apply information and skills. Most people think that the smarter a person is—that is, the higher his or her IQ—the more successful the person will be. Years of research, however, have proven that this connection often does not hold up.

As cited in O'Neil (1996), Daniel Goleman defined emotional intelligence as "...a different way of being smart. It includes knowing what your feelings are and using your feelings to make good decisions in life. It's being able to manage distressing moods well and control impulses. It's being motivated and remaining hopeful and optimistic when you have setbacks in working toward goals. It's empathy; knowing what the people around you are feeling. And it's social skill—getting along well with other people, managing emotions in relationships, being able to persuade or lead others" (pp. 6-11).

In addition to Goleman's work, there is an abundance of research (Bradberry & Greaves, 2009) suggesting that people with high emotional intelligence are more successful, both personally and professionally. In addition, they make everyone around them better. In fact, others gravitate toward them because of their ability to empathize, control their impulses, make thoughtful decisions, and work collaboratively. These are people you want on your team. Table 1.1 lists common behaviors in physical education and sport that are associated with either low or high emotional intelligence.

In reviewing table 1.1, think of how often the behaviors associated with low emotional intelligence are punished and how much time is used in resolving the resulting conflicts. Students and athletes who engage in these behaviors can drag a team down and cause great frustration among the people around them. In addition, it's often much harder to connect with these students; however, feeling connected is often what they need more than anything else.

Therefore, your goal as a teacher or coach should be not only to help young people master content and skill but also to help them with the journey of moving toward mastery and success. In fact, your primary focus should be on the

Table 1.1　Behaviors Indicative of Low or High Emotional Intelligence

Low emotional intelligence	High emotional intelligence
Becoming adversarial and arguing with a teammate who has an opposing opinion: *"You are lying! Your serve was out, and you know it. I'm telling the teacher!"*	Agreeing to disagree and calmly working toward a solution: *"It's obvious that we disagree. Let's think of a fair way to handle this. How about rock, paper, scissors?"*
Acting out in anger or frustration at an unexpected change: *"You told us we would get to play in the gym today! It's not fair!"*	Demonstrating flexibility: *"I was really looking forward to playing in the gym today. I hope we'll be able to use it tomorrow."*
Showing jealousy of others: *"The only reason she made the team is because her dad is friends with the coach."*	Recognizing and praising the efforts of others: *"You are such a hard worker. Congratulations on making the team."*
Blaming or giving up in the face of adversity: *"It's not my fault we lost. If you guys could actually hit the ball, maybe we would finally win a game."*	Demonstrating optimism and determination in the face of adversity: *"It's obvious that we're struggling. We can pull through this together. Every team has to work through tough times."*
Losing one's temper when an official makes a bad call: *"That ref doesn't know what he's doing! He must be blind!" (These comments result in a penalty.)*	Showing self-control in frustrating or intense situations: *(Say nothing.)*
Using excuses to get out of work or cover up mistakes: *"I couldn't get my 100 shots in. My sister took my basketball to a friend's house."*	Being resourceful when a problem or challenge occurs: *"Can I please borrow your basketball for an hour? My ball isn't here, and I need to get in my 100 shots."*
Blaming or making excuses when mistakes are made: *"I didn't hit her with the ball. She moved into my way right when I threw it. It's her fault!"*	Owning and taking responsibility for mistakes instead of making excuses or blaming others: *"I'm sorry I hit her with the ball. I wasn't paying attention. I'll be more careful next time."*
Reacting poorly to others' emotions: *"I can't believe he's crying just because he lost the game. What a baby!"*	Showing empathy and compassion toward others: *"Your team played hard."*
Getting defensive when provided with constructive criticism: *"She told me that I need to bend my knees more. She doesn't know what she's talking about!"*	Welcoming constructive criticism: *"What can I do to improve my shot?"*
Devaluing teamwork or collaboration: *"I don't need your help. I can figure it out myself."*	Appreciating the importance of teamwork and collaboration: *"We can do this. Let's figure it out together."*
Fearing failure: *"I can't do that. It looks too hard."*	Being willing to step out of one's comfort zone and try new things: *"It looks tough, but I'll do my best."*

process of mastery and development. Students succeed at much higher rates in mastering both skill and content when they are taught *how* to learn and improve. This approach includes teaching them how to learn from failure and work through obstacles. Fortunately, emotional intelligence can be strengthened and learned into adulthood.

The distinction between a growth mindset and a fixed mindset informs a popular theory used by schools, businesses, and athletic teams to help individuals positively work through frustration and failure. Psychologist and author Carol Dweck states in her many publications and workshops that people with a growth mindset "believe that their most basic abilities can be developed through dedication and hard work—brains and talent are just the starting point. This view creates a love of learning and a resilience that is essential for great accomplishment" (2006-2010, para. 4).

Thus people who have a growth mindset recognize that failure provides an opportunity to learn and improve; in contrast, people with a fixed mindset fear failure and tend to shy away from challenges. They give up more easily and make excuses when they experience failure. They are set in their ways and feel that their strengths and weaknesses cannot be changed through effort. By developing a growth mindset, students come to recognize and embrace the factors that contribute to growth, learning, and, ultimately, success.

FOSTERING UNDERSTANDING AMONG STUDENTS

The first step in helping students develop a growth mindset—and generally strengthen their emotional intelligence—is to deliberately teach the traits of emotional intelligence. Resources for building character are provided by many great character-education programs, but the best way to develop these valuable life skills is through an integrated approach. For example, toddlers learn to speak their native language through the integrated approach of constantly hearing words used in context. In other words, they don't learn the word *ball* because it is the "word of the week" that their parents teach them; they learn it by making connections every time they hear the word and see a ball. Making such connections strengthens learning.

Teachers and coaches need to take advantage of the many learning opportunities integrated into physical education and sport that connect naturally to emotional intelligence and a growth mindset. One way to do this is to continually praise students for demonstrating specific desirable skills, actions, and behaviors. Perspectives vary regarding the power of praise, as well as when and how to use it appropriately. In an article titled "The Perils and Promises of Praise," Carol Dweck states "The wrong kind of praise creates self-defeating behavior. The right kind motivates students to learn" (2007, pp. 34-39).

Rather than praising on the basis of ability or final outcome, it is much more effective to praise specific behaviors that contribute to emotional intelligence and a growth mindset, such as effort, risk taking, compassion, and inclusiveness. Focus on the behaviors that contribute to the process of learning and growing. In addition, recognize and praise specific positive character traits. In doing so, you reinforce the desired actions and attitudes. Here are some examples:

- "Harun, I noticed that you encouraged your teammates after your first loss. Way to go!"
- "Samariah, you looked a little frustrated after your team lost, and I'm impressed with how you handled it. You didn't get angry with anyone or quit. You went right back out there and worked even harder. What a great example of perseverance!"
- "This class does such a nice job of including others. Whenever anyone is left out, you invite him or her to join your group. What a great example of compassion and inclusiveness."

In order to be effective, praise must be genuine and honest; indeed, false praise can reduce trust. It's always nice to hear a heartfelt "good job," but specific praise about behavior, effort, and attitude is a much more effective teaching tool than generic praise.

Another way to integrate emotional intelligence into every lesson or practice plan is through the practice of reflection. Inviting students to make connections and think about how their actions affect their performance, and the performance of others, is an excellent way to learn. To help students engage in this kind of higher-level thinking, which reinforces and deepens their learning, ask them questions such as the following: "What did you learn today as a result of a mistake that you made? What do you need to do in order to improve?"

Depending on the current theme or focus, you can also ask inviting questions at the end of each class, such as, "What specific acts of integrity did you notice in class today?" This question allows students to connect the meaning of the word *integrity* to specific acts of integrity performed by their peers. Similarly, during cool-downs, pair students up and give them a reflective question to discuss, such as, "While you're cooling down, work with your partner to generate three examples of how encouragement was demonstrated in class today."

Unfortunately, many students do not know how to reflect, because they are rarely, if ever, given the opportunity to do so. Instead, they are told what they need to do in order to improve, which in many cases goes in one ear and out the other because the teacher or coach is doing the thinking. The best learning comes when students do their own thinking, reflecting, and connecting. In addition, reflective learners are much more likely to learn from their mistakes and avoid making them again.

Promoting Social Justice and Preventing Bullying

Just as inequities exist in the larger community, they also exist in the gym and on the playing field. Imagine, however, creating a classroom climate in which all students feel significant and cared for—regardless of their athletic ability, their weight, or the quality of their basketball shoes. By purposefully teaching students how to trust, accept, and care for each other, you can build a community of learners who feel connected and safe, both physically and emotionally. When students feel safe and connected, they are more likely to take risks, be honest about their thoughts and feelings, and trust those around them. Isn't this the best possible antidote to bullying and entitlement?

Physical education often provides the perfect environment for bullies. Ironically, it's also the perfect environment for bullying prevention. In the United States, bullying has gained national attention and as a result, bullying awareness is now part of curriculums in most school districts nationwide. Addressing bullying prevention in isolation is not always an effective approach. It is much more meaningful to integrate bullying prevention into subject matter by proactively teaching the desired skills and allowing students to apply those skills in a natural setting. When potential bullies learn how to be caring, supportive teammates as well as respectful competitors, they are able to choose positive alternatives in dealing with their negative intentions or feelings. In Donna Walker Tileston's book *Ten Best Teaching Practices: How Brain Research and Learning Styles Define Teaching Competencies* (2011) she writes:

> All of us want to belong somewhere. We want to feel we are a part of the experience and that we are accepted. When students do not feel accepted, for whatever reason, they are more likely to find negative places to belong. That is what helps keep gangs active in our students' lives. Gangs and other negative influences fill a need that so often is not met in positive settings. As educators, we must create an environment in which students feel safe and accepted, an environment in which we are all learners together and where we feel a sense of togetherness—one where there are no "gotchas." Students are told up front what they must do to be successful, and then we must be faithful and hold them only to the criteria that we set. (p. 13)

In an effort to understand human behavior, researcher Abraham Maslow's established "Hierarchy of Needs" way back in 1943. His five-stage model includes needs that ensure survival and drive motivation. Since then, many notable psychologists and researchers have used and contributed their own views to Maslow's research but very little has changed. Through this research, it's clear that a sense of belonging and significance are essential needs that drive motivation and behavior. These basic needs are often compromised in victims of bullying, where negative self-esteem and depression occur at higher-than-average rates. Students who are more athletic and physically fit may feel a strong sense of significance in settings associated with sport and physical education. But how do students who are uncoordinated or overweight feel? These students often fall victim to bullying or act as bullies themselves to gain their perceived significance. It's more likely that these students will lack the motivation to exercise or stay fit due to their negative experiences in physical education or athletics. These are the students who desperately need to feel a sense of connectedness, instead of shame and embarrassment that can sometimes result in physical education settings. In order to change the fitness and health trends, such as childhood obesity and disease and social acceptance, we must facilitate a feeling of significance and belonging in all youth, regardless of athletic ability, race, or socioeconomic status.

The best teachers and coaches recognize and build on the strengths of all participants. They send a message that everyone brings something to the table and has the ability to contribute to the greater good. When children learn how to recognize the strengths in others—as well as embrace diversity and celebrate differences—they are less likely to discriminate or develop the entitled feelings that so often exist in children who grow into bullies.

The key concepts and actions emphasized in this discussion—such as character education, emotional intelligence, community building, and social justice—share the following foundational components: compassion, empathy, respect, and acceptance. These elements apply both to the diverse world at large and to the smaller communities found in schools and youth teams. As Nelson Mandela once said, "Education is the most powerful weapon which you can use to change the world." Teachers and coaches need to recognize the effects that they have on the many young lives they influence every day. Teaching children how to be supportive teammates and respectful competitors is a great first step in equipping them with the necessary skills to embrace diversity and serve as positive contributors to a socially just world.

FACILITATING STRATEGIES FOR SUCCESS

In discussing the strategies of success, we focus on the experiences and situations encountered along the journey of learning. Most journeys include setbacks and sacrifice. Growth and learning can be joyful and rewarding, but it can also be frustrating and confusing. By facilitating strategies to help students gain success and provide them the tools to deal with the setbacks, students will begin to welcome challenges and be less likely to give up when their journey reaches a roadblock.

Setting Goals

Goal setting is closely linked to emotional intelligence and a growth mindset. More specifically, setting and accomplishing goals requires traits such as determination, self-awareness, motivation, self-control, and grit. In practice, however, students and athletes are often asked to set goals without being taught the valuable skills that can help them reach those goals. In other words, too much time is often spent on goal setting and not enough on goal *getting*.

Goal setting is one of the most widely used practices in sport settings, schools, and the workplace. If done correctly, goal setting can motivate students and athletes to maximize their performance. In many cases, however, goals are set and then left alone. Teachers and coaches may have the best of intentions when they ask their students, athletes, and teams to set goals, but as time goes on, those goals are often neglected or forgotten.

As mentioned earlier in the chapter, we need to make *process* the focus of learning and growing, and the same holds true for setting and achieving goals. Reaching goals involves an emotional journey that requires hard work, discipline, and sacrifice. Students have a much greater chance of succeeding in that journey if they understand how to overcome the inevitable obstacles they will encounter along the way. Growth is often associated with some degree of adversity, and one key factor in overcoming adversity is self-confidence. Indeed, believing in oneself is the first step toward achieving a goal and working through the frustration often encountered in the process. Students who lack self-confidence are much more likely to give up when faced with an obstacle because they don't believe that they can overcome it.

Therefore, building self-confidence in your students should be a top priority. You need to help students believe in themselves by first demonstrating that you believe in them. In discussing the importance of instilling confidence in youth, Joel Johnson, associate coach for the University of Minnesota women's hockey team, offered the following thoughts: "Confidence comes first from a proper and balanced outlook on life and sports. Young players, especially, need to know that their identity and self-worth doesn't come from their athletic success but from living a life of integrity, character, and striving for excellence in all they do" (Minnesota Hockey, 2016).

When examined closely, the phrase "striving for excellence" is strong language. As teachers and coaches, we need to be deliberate in teaching students what it means to strive for excellence and what behaviors are involved in doing so. This teaching begins with modeling and facilitating a growth mindset and involving students in their own learning. In this approach, making mistakes no longer contributes to negative self-esteem because students recognize it as a valuable part of striving for continuous improvement and reaching goals.

Using Assessment as a Tool for Growth

Assessment is often used simply as a tool for measuring, not as a means for motivating. When used more appropriately, however, it can serve as a powerful tool in the process of learning, improving, and achieving goals. As with goal setting, when students or athletes are actively involved in their learning, they become much more invested in the process and motivated to do their best. More specifically, both self-assessment and peer assessment can nurture a growth mindset and emotional intelligence traits such as embracing challenges, welcoming constructive feedback, honesty, reflective thinking, and self-discipline. In addition, when students are taught how to correctly self-assess and peer-assess, their learning is strengthened and their personal growth occurs at a faster rate.

Typically, as a teacher, you are in control of assessing students' progress. Put simply, you hold all the power and do all the thinking, and it can be difficult to consider giving up some of that control. Doing so, however, offers substantial benefits because the person doing all the thinking is the one doing all the learning. When students develop the ability to look more deeply at their work or progress—to reflect on it and assess it—they engage in higher-level skills such as critical thinking and problem solving. These are two of the most-desired skills in the 21st-century workplace.

When students assess their own work, they first analyze their progress and compare it with the stated goal or criteria. Next they create a plan for moving forward. Did they meet the criteria? If so, what are the next steps for continued growth? If not, what steps need to be taken in order to meet the criteria? These skills—analyzing, evaluating, and creating—are essential to being a critical thinker and to achieving goals and succeeding in a world of constant change.

Peer assessment requires the same critical thinking skills used in self-assessment, as well as the skills of collaboration and empathy, both of which are also highly sought after in the working world. In addition, when students work with a peer in either evaluating progress toward a goal or assessing a particular skill, they experience both support and accountability. Both self-assessment and peer assessment are excellent teaching and learning tools and highly motivating techniques. If poorly facilitated, however, they can also be completely ineffective and even disastrous. If you do not proactively teach a growth mindset, as well as the aspects of emotional intelligence needed for self-assessment and peer assessment, students will be left frustrated and will miss out on learning the skills needed in order to maximize their potential.

PREPARING STUDENTS FOR COLLEGE AND CAREER

Having a growth mindset and strong emotional intelligence are key to success in the gym and on the field. These traits are also necessary for excelling in the world at large. To help students and athletes maximize their performance, teachers and coaches must understand the factors that contribute to success and the qualities needed in order to be successful, most of which are outlined in this chapter. That understanding can be developed in part with help from the Positive Coaching Alliance (PCA). One of the most influential forces in youth and high school sport today, PCA is a national nonprofit organization dedicated to developing "better athletes, better people" by "...providing resources for youth and high school sports coaches, parents, administrators, and student-athletes...that help...create a positive, character-building youth sports culture" (www.positivecoach.org/mission-history, para. 1). PCA recognizes the value that sport can and should add to kids' lives, and the organization is transforming beliefs and philosophies among parents and coaches across the country.

Of course, the win-at-all-costs mentality still exists, but it is increasingly viewed as unacceptable, both in sport and in life. Instead, the emphasis has shifted to character building, and winning is more often approached as a secondary goal. Thanks to organizations such as PCA, more and more coaches are recognizing that their teams have a better experience—and a better chance of winning—when athletes feel cared about, respectfully challenged, and emotionally connected.

Physical education teachers need to follow suit. By teaching students how to set and reach goals and how to be respectful competitors and supportive teammates, you are setting them up for success far beyond the gym. Many physical educators are lobbying for daily physical education classes due to the increase in childhood obesity and disease. The negative health trends are not going to improve simply by providing increased daily activity. The trends will improve only if students are taught *how* to lead healthy lifestyles. In order to make a case for daily physical education, teachers need to demonstrate the many ways in which physical education can positively impact lives physically, socially, and emotionally. Physical education is the best possible subject in school to promote healthy lifestyles. The concepts associated with teamwork, competing with integrity, and goal-setting naturally develop leaders and build career-readiness skills.

A study featured on the LinkedIn Official Blog by Allison Schnidman (2014) highlighted the top traits desired by Fortune 500 companies. Allison and her team asked over 1,400 hiring managers from Fortune 500 companies in the

United States to rank which skills and personality traits they consider to be the most important when hiring young professionals.

The results indicated the following as the top skills desired in young hires:

1. Problem solver: able to see and create solutions when faced with challenges
2. Good learner: able to learn new concepts quickly, adaptable

And the top personality traits desired were identified as the following:

1. Collaborative: works well with others; good team player
2. Works hard: has strong work ethic; goes above and beyond
3. Positive attitude: demonstrates optimism; maintains positive energy

Physical education teachers and sport coaches need to lead the way in facilitating these skills in students and athletes; there's a natural connection.

SUMMARY

Physical education and sport need to lead the way in facilitating the development of emotional intelligence and a growth mindset in students and athletes. Imagine if student-athletes learned how to set and reach small, attainable goals on both the individual and team levels at a young age and then built on those skills each year. Imagine if they embraced their mistakes and recognized them as a valuable part of learning rather than quitting or giving up when frustration sets in. Imagine if teammates learned how to support each other by providing genuine praise and encouragement. Kids are capable of so much more than they are often given credit for. If we help children and adolescents take baby steps, nurture these skills, and then build on them throughout high school and college . . . just imagine!

This chapter outlines many of the skills necessary for success both on and off the field. The remainder of the book provides a road map to help you, as a teacher or coach, facilitate these skills by integrating them into your daily lesson plans and your interactions with students and athletes.

REFERENCES

Bradberry, T., & Greaves, J. (2009). *Emotional Intelligence 2.0.* San Diego, CA: TalentSmart.

Dweck, C. (2006-2010). What is mindset. Retrieved from http://mindsetonline.com/whatisit/about/index.html.

Dweck, C. (2007). The perils and promises of praise. *Educational Leadership, 65*(2), 34-39.

Minnesota Hockey. (2016, February 23). How to instill confidence in your player. Retrieved from http://www.minnesotahockey.org/news_article/show/614179?f5tp=1&referral=rss&referrer_id=710946.

O'Neil, J. (1996). On emotional intelligence: A conversation with Daniel Goleman. *Educational Leadership, 54*(1), 6-11.

Positive Coaching Alliance. (2016). Mission & history. Retrieved from www.positivecoach.org/mission-history.

Schnidman, A. (2014, October 10). What it takes for a young professional to get hired today. [LinkedIn Official Blog]. Retrieved from https://blog.linkedin.com/author/a/allison-schnidman.

Tileston, D.W. (2011). *10 Best teaching practices: How brain research and learning styles define teaching competencies.* Thousand Oaks, CA: SAGE Publications Ltd. doi: 10.4135/9781483387277.

Building Community to Enhance Learning and Motivation

There is no better exercise for strengthening the heart than reaching down and lifting up another.

Jim Ditulio, physical education teacher

In order to maximize growth and achievement in students and athletes, trust must be established among all participants. The first step in fostering that trust is to build community and create a respectful environment in which all participants feel a sense of value and purpose. Research overwhelmingly indicates that when students and athletes feel emotionally connected to and supported by their teammates, they invest more deeply in the shared vision and goals of the program.

This chapter addresses

- the importance of developing a positive learning environment in which all students feel a sense of belonging and significance;
- techniques to develop a community of respectful, motivated learners, including Y-chart discussions, lessons in praise and encouragement, and greeting and warm-up activities;

- unique ways to organize your class; and
- strategies to strengthen community through team names, pacts, posters, and cheers.

The chapter also provides activities to help you build a community of learners who accept, value, and trust each other. In order to establish such a community, you must create a positive, supportive learning environment.

DEVELOPING A POSITIVE LEARNING ENVIRONMENT

We all have a basic need to feel that we belong. When we feel a sense of belonging, and a sense of significance, we are much more motivated and invested in the experience. You can set students up for success in group settings by proactively anticipating problems and finding solutions to those problems before they arise. This approach not only helps avoid conflict but also teaches aspects of emotional intelligence, such as impulse control and conflict resolution skills. As a result, students will be more successful and productive while working in groups.

Working collaboratively is essential in the world at large; however, one major cause of conflict in the classroom is the practice of asking students to form groups or pick a partner without first teaching them how to do so. This scenario often results in hurt feelings, arguments, goofing around, and a frustrated teacher. As teachers, we cannot assume that students come to us already possessing the necessary skills of working together. Therefore, rather than getting frustrated with students for not having these skills, we need to help students develop them.

The many skills needed for successful group work include communicating with and supporting others. Working with others not only helps students develop their teamwork skills but also enables them to feel a sense of connection. In turn, when individuals trust and feel connected to those around them, they can take risks and step out of their comfort zones, thus enabling them to experience their greatest possible personal growth. We must facilitate this trust and connection among our students by teaching them how to work together respectfully and collaboratively.

During the first week of class, students need to learn what makes a good team member. To keep things fresh, use a variety of engaging group methods to help students construct the meaning and importance of teamwork.

Using Y-Charts

One popular way to teach social and emotional skills is by using a Y-chart (see figure 2.1). To use a Y-chart most effectively, divide the class into small groups of two or three members each. The first concept to address with the chart is teamwork, and the purpose of beginning in small groups is to account for the fact that students may not yet fully understand how to be a good teammate.

To begin the activity, assign each small group a piece of the Y-chart. In other words, each group brainstorms only for its assigned portion of the chart—what teamwork either looks like, sounds like, or feels like. Because the class will probably include eight or nine groups, each portion of the chart will probably be

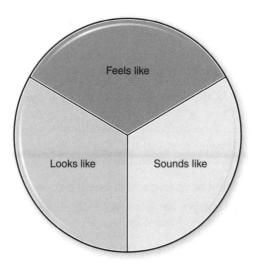

FIGURE 2.1 Y-chart.

addressed by more than one group. Give the groups three to five minutes to complete the task, then have them report their reflections to the entire class. Write the responses on a Y-chart displayed on chart paper and hang the finished chart in the room to serve as a constant reminder of what teamwork looks, sounds, and feels like.

Sample Y-Chart Progression: What Is Teamwork?

Teacher: "For the groups that brainstormed what teamwork [looks, sounds, or feels] like, what did you come up with?"

Here are some possible responses:

- Teamwork looks like people close together, uniforms of the same color, and high fives.
- Teamwork sounds like phrases such as "nice pass" and hand slaps from high fives.
- Teamwork feels like a sense of belonging, friendship, and happiness.

The next step in teaching positive teamwork is to address what it means to be a supportive teammate. Elicit detailed discussion by asking students to elaborate on selected responses. Also, ask students to describe specific examples of classmates demonstrating positive traits; this is a great way to reinforce those desired behaviors. You can incorporate this sort of reflection at the end of each game or activity. For example, you might ask, "What are some specific examples of teamwork demonstrated in the game we just played?"

Practicing Teamwork

Have students work in pairs or threes to brainstorm responses to the following questions (one question at a time).

> Teacher: "You've learned what teamwork looks like, feels like, and sounds like. Today, you have an opportunity to practice what you've learned by working in groups of two or three. In your groups, determine at least five characteristics of a good team member."

After the groups finish brainstorming, allow two or three minutes for students to share responses with the whole group.

To continue to strengthen students' understanding of what teamwork looks like, sounds like, and feels like, ask one of the following questions at the beginning of class throughout the first month of school:

- What does listening have to do with being a good team member?
- Think of teams that you've been part of. What traits characterize the teammates that you have most enjoyed?

After giving students time to think, either individually or with a partner, ask them to share their responses with the rest of the class and encourage discussion on each topic. As students share their answers, write their responses on a piece of chart paper to be hung in the gym.

To expedite the process, ask students to write their responses during the first class meeting, then discuss them during the next class meeting. This way, students will have more time to participate in physical activities. To integrate movement, pair students up, present a question, and have them do their warm-up or cool-down while sharing their responses. This time can be referred to as "walk-and-talk," "run-and-reflect," or "jog-and-jabber."

Students should also be given an opportunity to write individually about what kind of teammates they are. Ask students to respond to the following questions either in their fitness journals or on a separate piece of paper.

- What kind of teammate do you think you are?
- What are some of your positive characteristics?
- What are some areas you need to work on?

As part of this process, teach students that no matter how good they are at something, they can always improve. In doing so, you teach the emotional intelligence trait of self-awareness by encouraging students to be honest with themselves about their strengths and weaknesses and to identify ways to improve. This ability to engage in self-reflection is an important life skill. Remind students that one's quality as a teammate has nothing to do with one's athletic skills.

These same questions need to be asked at the end of the year to help students determine whether they have grown. Assure students that they don't have to share their answers with the whole group, but remind them that they do need to be honest about their teamwork skills.

Providing Opportunities for Reflection

Reflection is one of the most powerful tools for both teaching and learning. More specifically, it is crucial in establishing a growth mindset and developing emotional intelligence. By reflecting, students compare their actions with desired outcomes, criteria, behaviors, or skills. As students learn specific skills, you can use reflection to reinforce the positive behaviors that they demonstrate. By prompting students to reflect on positive behaviors, you also encourage them to recognize the good in others.

Most students (and many adults) do not know how to reflect.

Students and teachers alike often do not realize that reflection is essential in learning from mistakes, addressing weaknesses, and building on strengths. One way to address this lack of awareness—and to reinforce desired behaviors—is to ask students a reflection question at the end of each lesson. Here is an example: "Who can provide an example of perseverance today?" As before, you can integrate this class reflection time into the cool-down period.

The following sample progression illustrates one way to teach students how to work collaboratively in teams or groups.

> Teacher: "Today you are going to work in groups of four. What are some potential problems that you may encounter while working in groups?"

Allow students to respond one at a time while you write responses on the board. Here are some common responses:

- Goofing around
- Some kids not doing any work
- Arguing
- Bossing teammates around

> Teacher: "Now that the potential problems have been identified, it's time to figure out how to solve them. That way, if you have a problem, you will know how to work through it together. I'm going to give each group one of the potential problem scenarios. In your group, discuss how you might solve your problem in a respectful way."

> "Team 1, how will you solve the problem of kids goofing around? Team 2, how will you solve the problem of teammates not doing their fair share of the work? Team 3, how will you solve the problem of teammates not getting along or arguing? And team 4, how will you handle teammates who are bossy?"

Allow four or five minutes for the groups to brainstorm their solutions, then give each group a chance to share its responses. After all groups have shared, have a couple of students role-play (with your support) a scenario illustrating how they might solve one of the problems.

USING ACTIVITIES TO TEACH PRAISE AND ENCOURAGEMENT

Praise is not only an excellent way to motivate students and reinforce their development of desired skills; it is also a powerful concept in itself to teach students and teammates. When students learn to recognize positive character traits in their teammates, they reinforce their own skills and learn how to think more optimistically. When one person praises another, he or she focuses on the other person's positive actions. What a gift—to be able to recognize the strengths of the people around you!

Too often, when people provide each other with feedback, its content is negative, which negatively affects the recipient and perhaps the whole group or team. Granted, there is a place for honest, constructive feedback, but leaders often underestimate how motivating specific praise can be. By teaching students how to praise, you equip them with a lifelong skill that will strengthen future relationships, both personal and professional.

As compared with praise, encouragement can be more difficult to provide, because it is often needed most when things are not going well; it can also be appropriate when an individual or team is about to take on a challenge. When things are not going well, it is natural for an individual to feel down or frustrated, and students need to learn that strategies are available for channeling their frustration in positive ways. In addition, when they understand the power of encouragement, they learn how to support others in difficult times or challenging situations.

Think of how often breakdowns occur among teammates when frustration sets in and how often students and athletes give up when they experience failure. Teaching encouragement gives them a way to develop a growth mindset when taking on challenges and allows them to recognize that failure provides opportunities for learning. The best leaders can remain realistically hopeful in trying times and thus engender spirit and courage in others. As with praise, when students know how to encourage others, they can enjoy healthier relationships and develop stronger leadership skills.

The important skills of giving and receiving praise and encouragement must be taught. When students learn to recognize and articulate the positive actions and behaviors of others, they nurture aspects of emotional intelligence, such as communication skill and optimism. In this process, we must take care to teach students *how* to praise specific positive behaviors exhibited by others; for instance, false or generic praise is often ineffective and can even produce negative results such as always needing or seeking approval.

An easy way to start on this path is to get yourself into the habit of recognizing and praising the desired behaviors you see in your students or athletes. It is highly motivating for students to hear what they did well, and you are modeling how to recognize the good in others. Again, if the goal is to create a caring community of learners who support one another, then teaching students how to praise and encourage must be part of the process.

Being a good teammate also requires skill. In order for students to understand *how* to praise and encourage, they must understand the purpose of encouragement. You can guide students toward this understanding with the following discussion questions for teaching praise:

- How do you feel when you accomplish a difficult task or do well on a performance or test?

- When you experience that kind of success, what do others typically say or do? How do you feel in response?

You may choose to use the following words to further clarify the meaning of praise:

> Teacher: "Praising others is a powerful skill. Not many people, especially kids, take the time to praise others. At the same time, we all love to receive praise. Praise involves recognizing positive character traits, behaviors, or actions of others and then *telling them*! All too often, we miss out on building our teammates up either because we don't know how to praise or because we simply choose not to. Think of how you feel when others praise you for an action or behavior. Now think of how often you praise others. If not too often, that's okay because you are now going to learn how to praise, and there will be plenty of opportunities to practice in physical education."

Ask students for examples of praise phrases. Responses might include, for example, "good job," "way to go," "you are a star," and "nice going."

> Teacher: "Those are great phrases, and we may feel good when we hear them, but you are going to learn how to praise *specific* behavior. For example, instead of just saying 'good job,' you might say, 'Good job, Toni. You made some really good passes today.' What specific behavior or action did I praise in that statement?"

> "Now, I am going to shoot a basketball, and I want you to look very closely at what I do well when I shoot. Then think of how you can provide specific praise about my form. Please make sure that the praise speaks to something I did well. Providing false praise can be hurtful and reduce our trust in each other."

Shoot the basketball (or substitute another skill that kids are working on); then give students an opportunity to provide specific praise. Responses might resemble the following:

- "Nice job, Mrs. Anderson. You used a great follow-through."
- "You did a nice job of bending your knees."
- "Way to go—it looked like you kept your eyes on the target."

Repeat to students the specific praise they provided about your performance. Going forward, at the end of each class period, invite students to provide specific praise to classmates regarding something that went well during the period. Alternatively, reflect on praise phrases that were used during the class period. These approaches ensure that students continually hear good examples of specific praise. The more you model and provide examples, the more natural the practice becomes for your students.

Using Positive Adjectives

The web resource for this chapter includes a list of positive adjectives. These are great words for your students to know, and it is worthwhile to post them in the gym. Then, each week, pick one student to receive praise. At the beginning of the class period, assign five students to be in charge of praising the designated student at the end of the period. Assigning praisers in this fashion will probably be necessary at the beginning of the year; toward the middle of the year, however, praising should start becoming habitual for many of your students.

Here are specific directions for this activity:

Positive Adjectives		
Kind	Neat	Strong
Nice	Happy	Active
Cheerful	Courteous	Honest
Clever	Inventive	Imaginative
Enthusiastic	Helpful	Patient
Bright	Thoughtful	Determined
Convincing	Wise	Creative
Independent	Humorous	Pleasant
Delightful	Calm	Confident
Friendly	Inclusive	Empathic
Tolerant	Funny	Caring
Compassionate	Generous	Outgoing

From L. Anderson and D.R. Glover, 2017, *Building character, community in care: a growth mindset in physical education web resource* (Champaign, IL: Human Kinetics).

> Teacher: "Today we will be praising Juan. The five praisers will be Tim, Maurice, Tywon, Jerry, and Rianna. Each of you will be in charge of choosing one positive adjective that you feel best describes Juan, along with the specific action or behavior that supports the positive adjective you chose. At the end of the class period, while we are stretching, you will be responsible for sharing your praise by saying something like the following: 'Juan, I think you are (positive adjective) because you (specific example).'"

Examples include:

- "Juan, I think you are friendly because you include others."
- "Juan, I think you are creative because you find ways to get open when we play basketball."
- "Juan, I think you are enthusiastic because you high-five your teammates after a basket."
- "Juan, I think you are cheerful because you always have a smile on your face."

When students are asked to give a reason to support the positive adjective, they are challenged to think more deeply and therefore learn how to provide specific, genuine praise.

For each week or class period, choose a different student to be praised; make sure to keep track of the rotation so that everyone gets a turn. Not only does this activity allow students to learn how to provide specific praise, but also it does wonders for the self-esteem of the student receiving the praise. After a student is praised by classmates, ask him or her how it feels to be praised. Students' responses show the positive effect; often, they say something like,

"I had no idea my classmates felt that way about me." Whenever emotions are connected to learning, the learning is strengthened. And after students feel what it's like to be praised, they are more likely to provide that experience for others by giving praise.

Praising Partners

Whenever students work in pairs, each partner should be responsible for identifying something that the partner did well and providing specific praise for it at the end of the activity. In addition, beforehand, always have this behavior modeled in front of the class by students who are comfortable with doing so.

At the beginning of the activity, you might say,

> "Today, you are going to work in pairs. Each person is responsible for identifying something that his or her partner does well and then providing specific praise for it at the end of the activity. The praise may include either a specific positive character trait or something that the person did well during the activity."

When the activity is over, take a moment (as you should do regularly) to model specific praise while making sure that it addresses something that students genuinely did well. For example, you might say,

> "Class, you did a nice job of working together today. I was especially impressed with how well you took turns practicing your shots. Now, you've had time to find something specific that your partner did well. Who would like to share specific praise about their partner with the class?"

Allow two or three students to share their praise in front of the class. Remind the students offering praise to look the receiver in the eye while sharing their specific praise. Students may offer statements like the following:

- "Way to go, Adrian—you did a nice job of rebounding your shot and then giving me a turn."
- "Nice going, Marco—you were very patient when I had to chase my ball across the gym."

Before you ask students to share their specific praise with their partners, ask them to identify the specific praise that was just shared about Adrian and Marco. Again, the more you reinforce the positive and invite students to make the connections, the faster they learn the concepts.

Receiving Praise

As with giving praise, we cannot assume that students know how to receive praise. You can begin addressing this skill by simply asking your students, "How should you handle it when someone praises you?" Students tend to respond by noting that one should say "thank you," and you can invite a student to come forward and model the process with you.

Teaching Encouragement

Use the following questions to guide students in a discussion about encouragement.

- Have you ever been frustrated in physical education or on a team outside of school?
- Without blaming teammates or putting anyone down, what are some situations that you have felt frustrated about?
- How did you feel when you were frustrated?
- What did others say or do that led you to feel worse?
- What did others say or do that led you to feel better?

> Teacher: "Whenever we try something new or challenging, it is very likely that we or others will make mistakes. When mistakes are made, or when things don't go the way we would like, frustration often results. The good news is that mistakes are an important part of learning and getting better."

Continue by posing the following question: "If you notice that one of your teammates is frustrated, what could you do or say?" Build off student responses by clarifying the purpose and importance of encouragement.

> Teacher: "Encouragement is all about building others up when they are down or when an individual or team is trying to do something that is challenging. It's helping others better understand a growth mindset. Sadly, when frustration sets in on a team, very few teammates know how to build their team up by providing encouragement. Too often, teammates get down on each other and say or do things that only bring the team down more. Therefore, it's a great skill to be able to encourage others."

Continue with the following questions:

- What is the definition of *encouragement*?
- How does it feel to be encouraged?
- How does encouraging others affect a team?
- In what situations might it be difficult to encourage your teammates?

After the students grapple with generating a meaning for the word, tell them that the dictionary definition is something along the lines of "to give courage to."

> Teacher: "Wow, think about how strong your team could be if you built each other up and gave courage rather than tearing each other down!"

Using Encouraging Phrases and Signals

Ask your students for some examples of encouraging things they could say to help a teammate grow stronger or work through adversity. Here are a few possible responses:

- "Keep going."
- "Give it another try."
- "Don't give up."
- "You can do it."
- "Let's work together."

Now ask students for nonverbal examples of encouragement. Responses may include the following:

- Thumbs-up
- Fist bump
- Pat on the back
- High five
- Smile

Write students' responses on a large piece of tagboard and post it in the gym as a reminder that encouragement can be both verbal and nonverbal. Place such reminders throughout the gym.

One simple way to practice encouragement is by engaging students in one of the team-building challenges covered in chapter 5. When taking on team-building challenges, students usually fail in their first few attempts. These failures provide great opportunities to teach a concept that is part of a growth mindset: Failure can help us become stronger if we choose to learn from our mistakes. The team-building challenges also provide opportunities for students to practice offering encouragement. When teams don't succeed right away, team members often get down. To address this tendency, assign students to act as encouragers and then reflect on the encouraging phrases used throughout the activity.

In fact, any time that students are engaged in an activity that you know may present a challenge, assign certain students to serve as encouragers. By midyear, it will be natural for your students to encourage others, and you will no longer need to assign the task to specific students. Continue, however, to reflect on encouraging phrases used throughout the year.

Once your students understand the purpose and importance of encouragement—as well as specific phrases that they can use—it's time to let them practice. Here are a couple of examples.

Eggbeater Example

Adapted, by permission, from D.R. Glover and L.A. Anderson, 2003, *Character education: 43 fitness activities for community building* (Champaign, IL: Human Kinetics), 36-37.

Four students turn the ropes, the fifth student jumps, and the sixth student serves as the recorder (see figure 2.2). Provide the recorder with a worksheet, a pencil, and a clipboard. The turners and the jumper rotate positions so that all the turners get a chance to jump. The recorder does not have to rotate. Students can also add the advanced skill of jumping with a short rope inside of the eggbeater.

During the activity, both the turners and the jumper practice their physical skills, but only the turners practice their praise and encouragement skills. The recorder notes the responses of praise and encouragement of the turners on a social skills observation sheet (see the web resource).

After the students have had time to practice the physical skill of rope jumping, bring them back into a large group for discussion. The recorders can now

FIGURE 2.2   Eggbeater.

The eggbeater activity was created by physical education teacher Debbie Vigil.

share their observations with the class, which not only gives students recognition for their social skills but also allows the class to evaluate what has occurred. You might also pose some of the following questions:

- Were any put-downs or criticisms used?
- How do put-downs leave you feeling?
- How did being praised lead you to feel?
- How were you encouraged?
- Was it hard to praise or encourage another person? Why or why not?
- Was it hard to receive praise or encouragement? Why or why not?

Social Skills Observation Sheet

Name	See	Hear

Basketball Example

Older students can practice praise and encouragement while practicing basketball skills. Specifically, while one student practices shooting, the rebounders and passers can practice praise and encouragement.

Set up five poly spots in an arc around the basket; the distance from the basket should be determined by the age of the students. Organize the students in the following manner.

- One student is designated as the shooter. The shooter's job is to make a shot from each poly spot within a three-minute span.
- Two students are designated as rebounders. Their job is to retrieve the ball after each shot and get it to one of two passers.
- Appoint two other students as the passers. Once a passer receives the ball, he or she passes it to the shooter for another attempt. This process continues until either the shooter makes a shot from each poly spot or the three-minute time limit is met.

During the activity, the rebounders and passers provide specific praise and encouragement to the shooter. Appoint another student (or two) per group to fulfill the role of recorder. As in the eggbeater example, the recorder's job is to note all specific praise and encouragement, verbal and nonverbal phrases, on the social skills observation sheet (see the web resource).

Have students perform as many rotations as you wish. (You may want to give everyone a chance to shoot.) You decide how to rotate shooters, but remember that the recorders do not rotate. After a set amount of rotations, bring the class together and have the recorders report all praise and encouragement that was noted.

Remember, with all of the practice examples, it is crucial to have students record the praise and encouragement offered and report it to the class. It is also crucial to have students reflect on and discuss the group's process, or what the group members did well together and where they need to improve. Just as an athletic team needs to periodically process its efforts, students who are learning how to be good teammates also need to process and reflect. Perhaps, asking reflective questions such as, "How did it feel to be praised or encouraged by your teammates?" and "How did it feel to offer them praise and encouragement?"

BUILDING COMMUNITY THROUGH TEAM STRUCTURE

Another great way for students to practice specific praise and encouragement, as well as teamwork skills, is through physical challenges. After implementing the preceding lessons for praise and encouragement, assign each group a team-building challenge. Purposeful team-building challenges foster a group's creativity and force group members to plan a strategy for solving the challenge. This process, of course, allows the group plenty of opportunity to communicate, organize, fail, reorganize, and try again.

Starting Class With Teams

To build community among students and athletes, teachers must move away from traditional methods of starting class or practice. Typically, upon entering the gym, students report to their squads, which are usually arrayed in a straight line that is convenient for the teacher. Unlike a team or circle formation, this approach to starting class or practice does nothing to encourage building relationships. If we take a different approach and begin class with students in teams, then students always have a group to belong to, which allows for greater connection among participants. The main reason for using the team structure is to strengthen relationships and provide students with a safety net immediately upon entering the gym. When you establish a smaller group setting and have students report directly to their teams, you create a safer, friendlier atmosphere.

Indeed, research has shown that having students begin class in a group of people with whom they feel comfortable and accepted is a crucial step in creating an ideal learning environment. Once you have decided the makeup of the teams, instruct students to report directly to their teams at the beginning of each class and sit (or stand) in a circle. This configuration facilitates communication and group spirit; more specifically, the advantage of a circle over a straight line is that students can look each other in the eye rather than looking at the back of each other's head. When everyone can make eye contact, a more welcoming atmosphere is created. In addition, in a circle, everyone is equal because no one is at the front or the back.

Teams can be assigned in about the second week of school, after students understand what teamwork looks like, sounds like, and feels like. Provide a game situation that allows students to practice teamwork. For example, you might say,

> "Now we are going to play a game. Can you put your words into actions? You stated that it is important not to put down your teammates or members of the other team. You also stated that you were going to involve everyone on your team. You have learned the importance of praise and encouragement. Now it's time to show what you've learned by demonstrating the behaviors you've described."

When the game is over, allow time for reflection. You might ask,

> "Who can provide specific examples of good teamwork today?"

To strengthen relationships, trust, and confidence, teams should stay together for at least a semester. After the third or fourth week of school, the ritual of reporting immediately to one's team becomes routine, and you will no longer need to instruct the students to do it. Together, the teams will participate in many activities that promote trust, acceptance, and support.

Team Setup

The team approach to class not only encourages community but also provides a time-efficient way to organize activities throughout the year. Teams should warm up and participate in the games and activities together as much as possible. An appropriate number for a team is six to eight students.

Team setup and naming can be handled in many fun and creative ways. To add some fun to this format, invite students to create their own team names instead of simply using numbers. For example, students might model their team names after those of college sport teams, such as the Gophers, Cornhuskers, or Lions. Team names must be positive; do not accept negative or demeaning names. You might invite the class as a whole to help determine a theme or category for team names; however, the names themselves should be left to each team.

To enable organizational efficiency, each team member can be assigned a role according to a specific sport. For example in basketball, each team could include the following roles: captain, guard, forward, center, coach, and praiser or encourager.

Because this organizational method establishes the same roles on each team, it creates efficient ways to organize various activities. Here are some examples:

- "Today, the team **captains** will start the warm-up."
- "All **guards** will be in charge of making sure that each teammate is enthusiastically greeted."
- "The **coach** on each team will be in charge of getting the equipment put away."
- "The **praiser** on each team needs to make sure that each team member is praised or encouraged during class today."

- "Today, all **centers** are going to switch teams and teach another team their secret handshake."
- "The reflection scenarios today will be facilitated by the **forwards**."

These are just a few examples of how this format contributes to organizing activities efficiently. Whereas the roles used here reflect basketball, you (or your students) can choose any sport on which to base team roles.

Team Pact

Adapted, by permission, from D.R. Glover and L.A. Anderson, 2003, *Character education: 43 fitness activities for community building* (Champaign, IL: Human Kinetics), 39-40.

Instruct each team to make a plan for being a successful team. The purpose of creating a plan, or pact, early in the team's development is to learn how to prevent problems and how to solve any that do arise (figure 2.3). This activity can be done during the second or third week of school. You can then identify consistencies among the team pacts and post them as "Our Class SOP" (standard operating procedure).

> Teacher: "Your team needs to come up with guidelines to ensure success. What needs to happen with each teammate for your team to function as positively and productively as possible? Think about what we have talked about the last couple of weeks. What have you learned about the characteristics of a good team member? With these questions in mind, go ahead and determine your guidelines. These guidelines are going to be called your 'team pact.' Once you have finalized your team pact and everyone

FIGURE 2.3

Team Pact for the Gophers

For our team to be successful, all members will adhere to the following rules (Be specific. For example, if you say that students must all respect each other, what does that mean? What behaviors show respect?):

- Do not use put-downs.
- Encourage teammates when they make a mistake, when they are down about something, and when they are doing something that is really hard.
- Praise teammates when they do something well.
- Listen to whoever is talking and don't interrupt.
- Don't always just sit by friends in huddle activities.
- Include everyone on the team, and be nice to everyone.
- Always high-five each other after class.
- Don't always be the one who has to go first.
- Find a fair way to make decisions.
- Help teammates solve problems.

agrees on it, each team member needs to sign it. Determine a fair way to designate who will be the recorder for your team."

In developing its pact, each team can be responsible for generating at least five guidelines.

Figure 2.3 shows an example of what a fifth-grade team might produce for its team pact. Once the pact is constructed and signed by all team members, post it somewhere in the gym that is available for easy reference. The following is an example of what a team pact might look like.

Another technique is to ask students what they need to do in order for their physical education class to be the best that it can be. Compile all of the answers on one big poster board and post it in the gym. Then ask students what the teacher needs to do in order for the class to be the best that it can be. Again, record all thoughts on a large board and post it in the gym.

After each lesson, ask students to reflect on what went well: "Who would like to give an example of positive teamwork that your team displayed while creating your team pact?"

Team Poster

The team poster can feature the team name and a colorful decoration or logo. Give the teams time to create a team poster during physical education class; alternatively, assign it as group homework or work with the art teacher or classroom teacher to provide the teams with time to create their posters in other classes. When the posters have been finished, use these positive team designs to decorate the gymnasium. Also ask students to reflect on what went well:

> "Who would like to give an example of positive teamwork that your team displayed while creating a team poster?"

FOSTERING ENTHUSIASM AND MOTIVATION

Being enthusiastic is not always easy. However, if we learn and teach specific techniques for demonstrating enthusiasm, our lessons will be more meaningful and motivating. As with every other skill that we want students to learn, enthusiasm must be taught deliberately. We cannot assume that students know what enthusiasm is or how to display it. In addition, enthusiasm must come from students themselves; we cannot make students be enthusiastic. We can, however, teach them specific methods for conveying enthusiasm. Try the following approaches in your classroom:

- Vary the way in which you speak; alter your pitch, tone, and volume. Use some excited speech if you want to fire up your students.

- Look students directly in the eyes when you talk to them. This conveys to them that you have an interest in what they are doing. Widen your eyes and raise your eyebrows to show excitement in their accomplishments.

- Use facial expressions to show your excitement about what you are presenting in your lesson. Remember one of the golden rules of growing up—smile!

- Express your own feelings—for example, your happiness or your disappointment.
- Encourage your students. All of your students need encouragement to be able to do their best. Encouragement is a way to instill confidence in your students.

From "Enthusiasm and Feedback: A Winning Combination" (2001) Monica Parson, from Elon College in North Carolina.

You can also have students construct definitions for the words *enthusiasm* and *motivation* with their teammates. Some students might then model enthusiasm while the rest of the class identifies the specific behavior indicating enthusiasm. You can also have students use a Y-chart to address what enthusiasm sounds like, looks like, and feels like. Encourage students to draw on their own experiences of being around an enthusiastic person, as well as the feelings that such experiences evoke in them.

After each lesson, ask students to reflect on what went well. For example, you might ask, "How did it feel to be greeted as you entered the gym today?" In addition, model enthusiasm as much as you can so that students can learn from your example.

Team Breaks and Cheers

Many teams at the high school, college, and professional levels use a huddle break and cheer. This ritual symbolizes a common bond and contributes to team spirit; in addition, the physical nature of using a huddle break to demonstrate team unity generates enthusiasm and excitement. Why can't we do this in physical education? Well, we can—and we should.

Consider this scenario: Students are in their teams, and you have just given them instructions for a warm-up or a game. Each team comes together in a small circle, and team members put their hands in the middle. Someone counts to three, and, in unison, the team yells its team cheer. The cheer could be something as simple as the team name or something fancier that has been created by members of the team. Using a team cheer before every activity—and exchanging high fives afterward—goes a long way toward developing a strong sense of community and a positive classroom atmosphere.

If you have examples of sport teams doing fancy cheers, show them to your students to give them an idea of the possibilities. You can also invite local high school athletes to model what their team does as a special cheer or handshake.

Elementary students can spend a bit more time coming up with their special cheers. In fact, this is a great activity for a language arts or drama class, as well as a fantastic way to connect physical education with other subjects. As part of this process, students can be invited to research existing team cheers; for example, perhaps a South Wales rugby team has a unique cheer that a student team could adapt for use in class. This activity fits in well with other disciplines at the elementary level because it allows for creativity in many ways. For middle school and high school students, however, it would have to be done in the physical education setting because team members often do not see each other in other classes. As a result, their team cheer or break may be less involved and much shorter.

After each of these lessons, ask students to reflect on what went well. For example, you might ask, "In what ways did your team support each other today?"

Motivators and Greetings on Arrival

Adapted, by permission, from D.R. Glover and L.A. Anderson, 2003, *Character education: 43 fitness activities for community building* (Champaign, IL: Human Kinetics), 27-30.

Greeting students on arrival is important in establishing a strong community. We define motivators and greetings as enthusiastic verbal and physical actions by which each student is recognized. To establish a sense of belonging and a feeling of significance for each student, we need to let all children know that their presence matters. Every child should have his or her name spoken in a greeting at least once during the school day, and it must happen in every physical education class meeting. The sense of being recognized needs to be experienced early in the class session to help students feel comfortable and connected and to help eliminate any fears that they may have about participating in physical education class.

The greeting can be handled either immediately as students enter the gym, in their team huddles, or in a large group as part of a warm-up. The main purpose is to help students feel welcomed and fired up for class. Another purpose is to help students learn how to acknowledge people in a friendly way and understand why it is important to do so.

To introduce greetings and motivators to your students, ask them how they would feel if they entered a room and everyone looked up at them—and then looked away. Next, change the scenario so that it ends with someone acknowledging them in a friendly way. This discussion helps students realize how their own actions can affect other people. Are they the students who would look away? Or are they the ones who would smile, make eye contact, and say hello?

Here are some examples of different types of motivators and greetings.

Teacher-Led Motivational Greeting

Stand at the door and high-five students as they walk in. Display an enthusiastic attitude while saying hello and addressing each student by name. Enthusiasm is crucial. If you want your students to be motivated for class, let them know that you're excited to have them there! Giving students a high-five greeting portrays your enthusiasm, especially when combined with a verbal greeting: "Hello, Max!" "Good to see you, Hannah!" "Welcome to class, Lin!"

As with the teacher-led motivator, the student-led motivator (addressed in more detail a bit later) also plays an important role in helping people feel welcomed and motivated. However, before students are allowed to take on this role, they must practice it with one another. Stress to students that they may not practice selective enthusiasm. Address these issues up front, and revisit them throughout the year.

Secret Team Handshakes

Invite each team to create a special handshake that is unique to its members. The handshake can include any nontraditional way of shaking another individual's hand; it can also involve the whole team simultaneously greeting each other in a distinct way. Teammates might also create a special team greeting for two or three members to use when passing each other in the hallway or seeing each other in the larger community. As always, remind students of their team pacts, which can provide guidance if conflict arises in creating the handshake. In fact, it is a good idea to review the pacts occasionally before teams engage in a collaborative activity.

After each of these lessons, ask students to reflect on what went well. For example, you might ask, "How did you make sure all teammates had an opportunity to share their ideas? How does it feel to have a team handshake?"

Team Greetings

In this greeting, one team stands at the door and high-fives students as they enter class. This fun greeting is similar to the introduction of starters at a basketball game, where team members line up and then run to center court as their names are called, high-fiving their teammates along the way. It also resembles a cheer. Instead of saying something like "Hello, Ava" or "Welcome, Josh," greeters use greetings such as the following: "Way to go, Ava!" "You're awesome, Josh!" "All right, Dani!" Students can brainstorm their own specific ways to cheer on their teammates. It's great if they get loud and crazy in this greeting, because we want students to be fired up for class!

When your students are ready to lead the greeting, this is the ideal one to start with. Students are more comfortable motivating others when they do so as part of their team rather than by themselves. In fact, you can expect them to be a bit quiet the first time their teams do the greeting, but don't worry—the more they get to know and trust those around them, the more enthusiastic they become.

Two-Team Greetings

This one can get *really* loud and crazy! But what a fun experience it is for someone who will never have the opportunity to be part of a team outside of school. This greeting is similar to the preceding one, but in this case, *two* teams stand at the door, one at each side. As students enter, they greet and high-five classmates on both sides. Again, the teams doing the greeting need to be encouraged to really get into it and cheer enthusiastically for their classmates as they enter the gym.

Specific Individual Roles for Greeting at the Door

You can help organize greetings by assigning specific tasks to individuals on each team. For example, you might say, "Today, all captains are in charge of serving as the greeters; tomorrow the guards will high-five their classmates." Remember to rotate the greeters and let students know their assignment ahead of time so they are mentally prepared and can station themselves at the designated greeting spot. You can also assign students in a specific team role to ensure that each team *member* is greeted. For example, you might say, "Today all forwards are responsible for enthusiastically greeting each teammate after everyone has reported to their team."

Student-Led Greeting

In this greeting, one student stands at the door and greets classmates in the same manner as in the teacher-led motivator. Do not appoint an unwilling student to perform this role; rather, give it to a student volunteer. In addition, before having students take on this role, discuss the attitude of the greeter with the class. As part of this discussion, you might model enthusiastic greetings with students and have them practice with each other. As a class, students can also brainstorm words and phrases to use as greetings so that the greeter has lots of options. Here are a few examples: "Hello, Jim!" "Good to see you, Harun!" "Welcome to class, Fatimah!"

The student's responsibility is to greet each classmate by name, as part of the phrase that he or she chooses. The student greeter plays an important role in helping people feel welcomed and motivated. Students should practice this role with each other before you allow them to perform it. Do not allow students to be enthusiastic when they greet some students but unenthusiastic when they greet others. Doing so defeats the purpose of the greeting and may hurt the feelings of others. Address these issues up front and revisit them throughout the year.

Follow the Leader

Give each team a chance to model its handshake; then direct the rest of the students to each use it in greeting three other people. For example, you might say, "Today, you are going to greet each other using team A's handshake. Team A, show us your handshake and greet your teammates in your most enthusiastic way, making sure to say the name of the student you greet." Team A then models its handshake while the rest of the class watches. Next, you might say, "Now, greet at least three other people using team A's handshake." Thus if the class includes five teams, students have five different handshakes to use as greetings.

Birds of a Feather

If teams are organized by team roles (e.g., coach, center), each person on a team should have a specific role. You might say, "Today, you will greet students who have the same role as you. For example, each center will enthusiastically greet all of the centers from the other teams."

LARGE-GROUP GREETINGS AND WARM-UP ACTIVITIES

Greetings should be unique and varied in order to keep them fresh and fun. To that end, instead of always having students greeted at the door or doing a secret handshake, try the following ideas. These fun activities serve as greetings as well as large-group warm-ups. Some require specific songs, which are available for download from common music websites.

Many of these activities also require students to work in pairs or groups, and, as discussed earlier, working together can present conflicts. If you are proactive, however, students will know what to do if someone is left out or the numbers are uneven. Even so, students may need to be reminded by being asked, "How are we going to handle it if someone does not have a partner?" Remember to recognize the specific behaviors of students who reach out to include others who are left out. Again, when desired behaviors are positively reinforced, students are more likely to engage in those behaviors.

I Will Find You

Equipment

- Favorite gym music
- Four plastic hoops
- Index cards, each bearing the name of a locomotor movement (e.g., skipping, galloping, walking, running, sliding, leaping, twirling, jumping, hopping, moving on all fours like a puppy, crab-walking, running zigzag, marching)—two cards for each exercise and one card per student

Description

Randomly place the index cards facedown inside one of four hoops located in the center of the gym. Have students line up around the outside boundaries of the gym. If you have a basketball court, they should position themselves around the outside of the court. If not, place a cone in each corner of the gym about 10 feet (3 m) from the wall to provide boundaries.

When the music starts, students begin jogging around the designated boundary. On your signal (e.g., whistle, clap, tambourine), each student jogs to the center, gets a card, jogs back to the boundary, and continues their jogging jour-

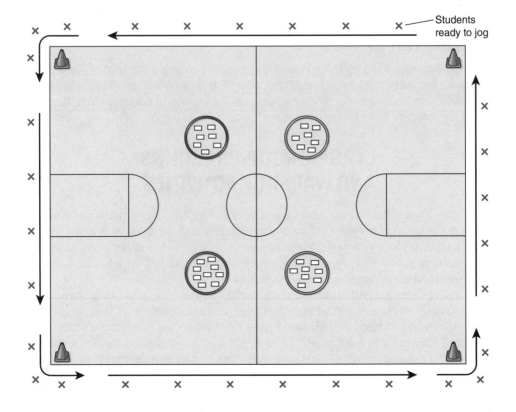

Students
ready to jog

ney. On your next signal, each student moves to the center in the manner indicated on his or her card and places the card in one of the hoops. Next, each student high-fives and greets the other student who moved in the same manner. Because the cards are made in pairs, everyone should have a partner to high-five; students may have to search for the correct person but should be able to find him or her. As with any new activity, brainstorm potential conflicts and solutions before they occur. For example, there may be an uneven number of students, in which case a student may not have a classmate to high five. If this happens, that student may high-five the teacher.

After the students high-five their partners, they each take a new card, return to the jogging path with the same partner, and again start jogging the gym or field. On your next signal, students each repeat the process by moving to the center hoops in the manner indicated on their new card, depositing the card, high-fiving and greeting their new partner (the one who moved to the center in the same manner *this* time), taking a new card, and jogging a lap around the outer boundary with the new partner.

Variations

- Put out four cards with the same movement instead of two. This approach allows students to greet and high-five more people in each round.
- Make sure that students take a card with a different movement each time. Instruct them to pick again if they pick up a card indicating a movement that they have already done.
- Add equipment. For example, provide a basketball for each student to dribble (or a floor hockey stick and puck to use) while moving and greeting.
- Instruct students to move in the way indicated on the card as soon as they pick it up (i.e., not just when returning to the center hoops).

Tambourine or Whistle

Equipment

- One tambourine or other means to loudly demonstrate a beat (e.g., whistle, clap)
- Favorite gym music

Description

Students gather in their teams and prepare to warm up. Instruct the teams that they do not have to stay together during this warm-up, because they will be forming new teams as the activity progresses.

Instruct the students to begin walking around the gym anywhere they would like to go as soon as the music starts. When the music stops, that is the cue for them to listen to the number of beats made by the tambourine (or other means). The number of beats indicates the number of students in each group; for instance, if you hit or shake the tambourine four times, then students get into groups of four. Once in their groups, each student must greet each fellow group member in a different way before the music begins again. For example, a student might greet one fellow member with a high five or high ten, another with elbow-to-elbow contact, another back to back, another knee to knee, and so on.

When you restart the music, the students disband and begin moving throughout the gym again, but this time they must move in a manner that differs from how they moved during the first round. When the tambourine signals again that it is time for students to form groups of a certain size, each student again greets each member of the new group in a different way. Continue this process until everyone has been greeted by several people and everyone is warmed up.

Variations

- Students ask new group members questions, such as, "What is your favorite food (or movie)?"
- After the members of a group greet one another, they must perform an exercise that you call out (e.g., 10 jumping jacks, 10 push-ups, 30-second hamstring stretch).

Hi and Move

Equipment

Favorite gym music

Description

Meet students at the door and explain that you have a new greeting and warm-up today. Tell students that they should come into the gym when the music starts and walk wherever they want to as long as the music plays. The only rule is that they must avoid contact with all other students. Then, when you pause the music for three seconds, they must high-five the closest person and say "hi" plus the student's name. As soon as you restart the music again, they once again move throughout the gym but this time in a different way (i.e., not walking) while still avoiding collisions. From there on, every time you pause the music, students must each greet someone, say "hi" plus the person's name, and then find a new way to move. Continue this process until everyone has greeted 10 classmates.

Variations

- Invite students to bring the music for the day.
- Have students greet as many people as they can with a high five before you restart the music.
- Make a playlist and have students greet every time the song changes.
- Have students change both the way in which they move and the speed at which they move after each pause.
- Keep the music playing continuously and have students greet a new person on your signal.

Agadoo

Adapted, by permission, from D.W. Midura and D.R. Glover, 2005, *Essentials of team building: Principles and practices* (Champaign, IL; Human Kinetics), 51-52.

Equipment

Recording of the song "Agadoo" and dance directions (from *Children's Party* by the Pop All-Stars, which is available for download on iTunes)

Description

This dance can be used from kindergarten through grade 12. It provides a great way to greet people and warm up. Class members can stand anywhere they

1. Agadoo-do-do
jab index fingers
forward 3 times

2. Push pineapple
pushing movement
forward with hands

3. Shake tree
clasp hands together swing
over left shoulder and right

4. Agadoo-do-do
jab index fingers
forward 3 times

5. Push pineapple
pushing movement
forward with hands

6. Grind coffee
make circles with hands
over each other
roly-poly movement

7. To the left
point left arm in
the air

8. To the right
point right arm in
the air

9. Jump up
both hands
in the air

10. And down
bring arms down
to knees

11. Cross over
hands at knees

12. Then bring
hands back

During chorus high-five as many people as you can before
verse starts, and when verse starts repeat dance.

choose within one half of a basketball court. When the music and singing begin, students perform the dance. When the dance verse stops and the chorus begins, students high-five and greet by name as many classmates as they can before the dance portion begins again. When the chorus starts for the second time, participants give double high fives and greet as many classmates as they can before the dance begins again.

You can choose a different greeting for students to use each time the chorus starts again. Each student must try to meet and greet as many people as possible during the chorus—that is, before the Agadoo dance starts again. Therefore, in order to keep up with the song, students must listen to the music while greeting so that they are ready for the Agadoo dance when it returns.

Variations

- Make the space either larger (e.g., entire gym) or smaller. This changes how much movement will be required—if you use the whole gym, students will have to jog.
- While greeting each other, have students learn the names and favorite foods of as many classmates as they can. How many can they remember?

Multiple Buddy

Equipment

Favorite classroom music

Description

The most important rule of this game is that students may not touch anyone except when greeting someone. Therefore, they must use their agility to avoid collisions. Start the music and instruct students how to move around the gym (e.g., run, skip, gallop, walk, hop). When the music stops, each student finds a person to high-five while saying his or her name. Each student must then remember that person as his or her high-five buddy.

When the music starts again, students begin moving in a different way, as instructed by you; as before, they do not touch anyone while moving. When the music stops again, they find a different buddy with whom they shake hands and say each other's name. Then they find their high-five buddy as quickly as possible and give him or her another high five before the music restarts.

This pattern can continue as long as you like. Each time the music stops, each student finds a new buddy, does what you instruct, and then finds all prior buddies in the correct order and performs the actions they originally did together. Examples of good buddy actions include double high fives, elbow-to-elbow contact, hip-to-hip contact, pinkie-to-pinkie contact, and so on. As always, you can also ask students for their ideas about possible buddy actions and let them take on the teacher role.

Variations

- Count down aloud from five before the music restarts after a buddy greeting. This approach adds excitement and challenge as students hurry to get all their greetings done before the end of the countdown, thus making it more difficult to avoid bumping into someone.
- Change the way in which students move around the gym each time the music restarts.

Pop Goes the Weasel

Equipment

Music for "Pop Goes the Weasel"

Description

Invite students to move about the gym as the music plays. You can either designate a movement or let them move however the music leads them to feel. On the first "pop," each student greets someone in the class with a high five. Afterward, students once again move around the gym until the next "pop," whereupon they each greet another person. This process continues for the remainder of the song, with each student greeting a new person on each "pop."

Variations

- Instruct students to move in a different way after each greeting.
- Have students use a different greeting on each "pop"—for example, a double high five, elbow-to-elbow contact, knee to knee, or back to back.

Foreign Language

Equipment

- Favorite gym music
- Poster with greetings in five languages other than English, such as the following:

  Hola (Spanish)

  Bonjour (French)

  Salute (Italian)

  Hallå (Sweden)

  Ahoj (Czech)

Description

Start the music and instruct students to begin jogging anywhere in the gym. Challenge them to see if they can use their dodging skills to avoid touching anyone else. After about one minute, stop the music and instruct the students to greet at least five people with a high five and a hello in another language (from the greetings poster). Next, challenge the students by asking, "Can you dodge to avoid collisions if we make the space much smaller?" Now move the students to half of the gym, restart the music, and let them jog and dodge in the smaller space. When you stop the music again, students must greet five *new* people with a foreign-language greeting and a high five.

Continually challenge the students to use their agility to avoid touching anyone. After a few minutes of using half of the gym, move the students into the space between the end line and the three-point arc (i.e., about one-fourth of the gym). Repeat the sequence. Now move the children inside the free throw lane; jogging and dodging in this small space can be very exciting—and challenging! Start the students moving very slowly, then increase the speed gradually; it is a very difficult task if you ask the students to move quickly in this small space. Remember to stop the music so that students can greet one another.

Variations

- Use a record player to change the speed of the music.
- To make this activity *much* more difficult, add changes in speed, level, or direction. You can also add equipment; for example, have students dribble a basketball while moving.
- Allow students to choose new ways to move each time you clap your hands.

Move Like Me

Equipment

Favorite classroom music with a strong beat and rhythm (e.g., a good dance tune)

Description

Scatter students around the gym; then start the music. Instruct the students to move around the area to the music in any way they like while avoiding contact with classmates. When you stop the music, each student finds a partner and greets that person with a gesture or movement that matches the syllables of his or her name. For instance, the movement for *Bob* might be a single hop or overhead arm thrust, whereas *Bobbie*, with its two syllables, would call for a movement on each syllable. The gesture or movement might involve something as large as a whole-body movement or as small as a single finger. In any case, the two partners show each other their movements, then put them together. Thus, for example, Bob and Bobbie would have a sequence of three movements performed one after another.

When the partners have learned each other's movements and put them into a pattern, restart the music. During this portion of the activity, each pair travels around the gym together. When you stop the music again, the partners find another pair with whom to share their movement pattern. The two pairs teach each other their movement patterns, thus giving each larger group a four-person pattern. The new groups practice their patterns for a few minutes in order to memorize them. When you restart the music, they perform their group patterns.

Variations

When the music stops yet again, have each four-person group partner up with another group of four. Now there is an eight-person pattern for all to learn, and these larger groups can use their longer patterns to move to the music.

Cowboy Slap Dance

Equipment

Music: "Cowboy Slap Dance" song (video of dance and music can be found on-line)

Description

This is a favorite elementary folk dance that has been used for years in physical education. We have changed it slightly to make it work as a mixer and greeter. It is great fun, although it can be hard in the beginning to keep up with the music; with practice, however, your students will get it.

Each student faces a partner, and the pairs are scattered randomly around the gym. When the music cues the movement, the partners pat each other's hands twice (fingers up, palms forward), then slap their own knees twice. They perform this sequence four times: hands pat pat, knees slap slap; hands pat pat, knees slap slap; hands pat pat, knees slap slap; hands pat pat, knees slap slap.

The partners then grab each other's hands and slide together: four slides in one direction, then four back to original spot. Next, they repeat this portion of the dance (four slides holding hands), but instead of then sliding back to the original spot, they quickly find a new partner and do an eight-count do-si-do with the new partner, and then start the dance all over with the new partner. Altogether, this sequence goes as follows:

1. Pat pat, slap slap: perform four times.
2. Slide in one direction for four slides, then slide back to original position in four slides.
3. Repeat slides, but instead of sliding back to original position, quickly find a new partner and do an eight-count do-si-do.
4. Do-si-do for eight counts with new partner. (If late getting a new partner, just start with pat pat, slap slap.)

Variations

- Students can swing the partner elbow to elbow instead of do-si-do.
- Have students do the dance in a line, with each facing a partner, then move to the next person in line when the time comes to find a new partner. (This approach makes switching much easier.)

Chicken Dance

Equipment

Music: "Chicken Dance" song (video of dance and music can be found online)

Description

Have students position themselves randomly around the gym. When the music cues them, they do the following steps:

1. Pinch fingers and thumbs together four times with hands at about shoulder height in front of body.
2. Flap arms up and down four times.
3. Wiggle body four times while bending knees.
4. Clap four times.
5. Repeat the sequence.
6. When the promenade music starts, high-five as many classmates as possible before the dance portion starts again.

The next time the promenade music comes on, students double-high-five as many classmates as possible before the music cues them to perform the dance movements again. The third time the promenade music starts, students greet others elbow to elbow, back to back, knee to knee, and so on.

Variation

Have the students change the way they move after each greeting.

Shoe Shuffle

Equipment

Favorite music for class

Description

Students form a large circle in the center of the gym. On your signal, they remove their shoes and toss them underhand into the center of the circle. When you restart the music, they walk around the gym. (Caution them not to run, which would pose a safety hazard without shoes.) Let them walk for several minutes, perhaps even interspersing exercises during this time: "Okay, stop walking, do 10 push-ups, and then start walking again." When the music stops again, students walk to the shoe pile and grab a right shoe and a left shoe—but not their own and not matching!

When you restart the music once again, students walk around the gym while holding their two chosen shoes. When the music stops this time, they try to find their own shoes, but here's the trick: The only way they can get a shoe back is to give the holder a high five, which releases the shoe back to its rightful owner. Of course, each student must readily give up a temporarily held shoe if someone approaches with a high five. Once a student retrieves both shoes, he or she resumes walking around the perimeter of the gym.

See how long it takes for everyone to get their own shoes back on their feet. Try it several times to give students a good warm-up in which they each greet several people.

Variation

Instruct students not to speak while seeking their own shoes.

Get That Name Right

Equipment

Peppy gym music

Description

Students stand in a large circle in the center of the gym and number off until everyone has a number. Then you call out five numbers, and the students with those numbers hustle to the center of the circle and stand in a straight line. When you hold your hand over the head of one of these five students, the class must yell out that student's name. This process continues for all five students in the center. When all five names have been recognized, start the music, which cues those five students to run around the circle giving everyone a high five. Then, the music continues while you call out five more numbers, thus calling those students to the center, and the process is repeated. This pattern continues until all students have been recognized.

Variation

Each time a group runs around the circle, the greeting method must be changed (e.g., elbow to elbow, double high five, handshake, fist bump).

Frozen Tag

Equipment

- Peppy music if you wish
- Six to eight colored vests or pinnies

Description

You may be familiar with the generic version of frozen tag, and this version closely resembles the original game except for the method used to "unfreeze" an individual who has been tagged. Choose one team to serve as the taggers; members of this team wear the colored vests or pinnies and are positioned behind one end line. The rest of the students are scattered around the gym. When the music starts, the taggers try to tag as many other students as possible. When a student is tagged, he or she must freeze in place with one hand extended. In order to become "unfrozen" (i.e., allowed to run again), the frozen student must receive a high five and be greeted by name by another student. Once unfrozen, the student must say thank you and the first name of the "unfreezer" before beginning to run.

Variations

- Change the method of unfreezing a runner (e.g., handshake, fist bump, double high five).
- Change the tagging team or use fewer taggers (e.g., half of a team).

Hoops

Equipment

- Four plastic hoops
- Favorite gym music

Description

After students have come into the gym and reported to their teams, place four hoops randomly around the gym. Instruct the students to move anywhere in the gym in any way they like when the music starts. Let the music play for about 30 seconds, then give a signal (e.g., whistle, clap, tambourine). On the signal, each student greets the nearest person with a high five while saying the person's name. Once they have greeted each other, they are now high-five partners who move together around the gym. After about a minute of moving together, give another signal, whereupon the high-five partners find another pair of high-five buddies to greet. Now there are four high-five buddies in one group, and they should stay together and continue moving around the gym.

The third time you give a signal, each group of four high-five partners finds another group of four and greets them. Once everyone has been greeted, the group of eight stays together and continues moving around the gym. After one minute of students moving in their groups of eight, stop the music and instruct each group to get into a hoop. Once each group of eight is positioned in a hoop, congratulate them all and say, "That was too easy for you." Then take away two hoops and start the process again. This time, all of the groups of eight must fit into just two hoops. Because class sizes differ, you may need to start with groups of three instead of pairs (or whatever works best for you).

Variations

- Have students start by jogging, then call out a new way to move when the signal is given.
- Require students to be connected in some way as they move throughout the gym.
- Require students in a group to stay connected when getting into a hoop.
- Use a giant team break and cheer when the warm-up is done.

TEAM WARM-UP ACTIVITIES

A warm-up serves a twofold purpose: to get the body physically prepared for class and to provide a fitness experiences that is fun and strengthens students' sense of community. The warm-ups presented here are performed in teams rather than in the traditional large group. This approach emphasizes developing team spirit and community.

While some of these warm-ups can be done in large groups, we advocate having student teams warm up together immediately following the team break and cheer. There may be days, however, when you want some variety or you want the teams to get to know other teams' individuals better. We do 90 percent of the team warm-ups in the students assigned team, but it's nice to change it up once in a while. For example, you might say, "All number 2s will participate in the warm-up together today," or, "For today's warm-up, all odd teams are together, and all even teams are together." Some of these warm-ups can also serve as the main activity for the day.

Spelling

As its name indicates, this warm-up not only teaches character-education concepts but also incorporates spelling. If you decide to do four rounds of this activity, you might use it as the main activity of the day.

Equipment

- Favorite gym music
- Plastic hoop for each team
- Fifty index cards (grouped into 5 sets of 10 marked by color for easy reference), with each card bearing a written letter and each set of 10 cards spelling one of the following 10-letter focus words: leadership, dedication, commitment, friendship, confidence
- Key showing the correct spelling of each word
- Poster of the focus words (to be hung on the wall in case younger students cannot figure out their word)

Description

Students gather in their teams around their assigned hoops on the outside of the gym (next to a wall). The 50 cards are placed randomly in the center of the gym or field. When the music starts, each team connects in some way (e.g., linking arms, holding hands) and stays connected while moving around the outside of the activity area. Instruct the teams to avoid touching the hoops while moving around. Every time you give a signal (e.g., hand clap, whistle, tambourine), each team must move in a different way while remaining connected. Let the students make at least three laps in this manner, which requires them to communicate and coordinate their movements while traveling.

When the music stops, each team disconnects, moves to the center of the gym, and collects a set of 10 cards. (Cards in the same set share the same color.) When ready, the team members carry the cards back to their hoop, put the letters in the hoop, and try to figure out their word. When they have ordered the letters to spell the word correctly inside of their hoop, they raise their hands to signal you to visit their hoop and check their spelling. If it is correct, the team then takes a couple of minutes to generate a definition for the word and prepares to report the word and definition to the class. If the word is spelled incorrectly, the teacher should walk away for a couple of minutes while the team attempts a new spelling before calling the teacher over again.

Variations

- Put the letters on 10 matching objects (e.g., tennis balls, softballs, basketballs, footballs). After spelling its word, each team must throw and catch the ball or make a certain number of baskets.
- Allow teams to walk and talk while figuring out a definition.
- If some teams have trouble figuring out their word, give a hint by showing them the focus-word poster.

Mirror, Mirror, in My Gym

Equipment

- Favorite gym music
- One gym mat
- Four cones

Description

Place the mat in the center of the gym. Place one cone in each corner of the gym, about 10 feet (3 m) from the wall; this setup provides a running track for the teams. If you would rather have students simply jog around the outside of the basketball court or around a field that will work just as well. Each team should gather somewhere on the running track, as far away as possible from other teams. Allow about five minutes for the teams to each create their own team formation. In making the formation, team members must be connected, and each person in the design must assume a different shape or figure.

After the teams have practiced putting together their formations, start the music, which signals the students to start jogging in their teams around the boundaries of the gym or field. When you stop the music, one designated team

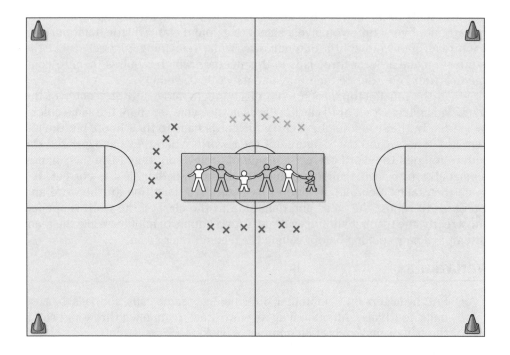

runs to the center mat and puts together its design; the other teams gather around and try to duplicate the formation. Once every team has accomplished the design, restart the music and instruct the students to return to jogging with their teams. When the music stops again, the next designated team runs to the mat and puts together its design for the other teams to duplicate. This process continues until all teams have been to the mat.

Tip: You might want to give the teams a minute or two to practice their designs after each round, since they may not remember their original creation.

Variations

- Add equipment (e.g., basketball, volleyball, tennis racket) to make the designs more interesting and harder to duplicate.
- Put two teams together to create a larger design for the others to duplicate.
- To make it *very* interesting, add chairs, cones, standards, or (if outside) trees.
- Add music and instruct students to make their designs move rhythmically to the beat.

Exercise Tag

Equipment

- Six pinnies or vests
- Six index cards, each bearing the name of an exercise and a number of repetitions to perform
- Any equipment needed for the six exercises (e.g., jump ropes)
- Favorite gym music
- Two or three gym mats

Description

Students report to the gym and sit with their teams. Select one team to serve as the taggers, who wear colored vests or pinnies with exercise cards affixed to them. Here are some appropriate exercise examples:

- Sit-ups (5)
- Push-ups (5)
- Jumping jacks (10)
- Windmills (10)
- Rope jumps (10)
- Squat thrusts or burpees (5)

On a signal (e.g., music starting), the team designated as the taggers tries to tag as many other people as possible. When tagged, a person must report to the mats, which are positioned along a wall outside of the tagging area, and they now have the opportunity to perform the activity indicated on the tagger's vest, after which he or she may rejoin the game. After a few minutes, allow a different team to serve as the taggers; members of the team that just finished its tagging stint should high-five each other.

Variations

- When a student is tagged, he or she has the opportunity to improve their cardiovascular fitness by jogging one lap before rejoining the game.
- Students use noodles for tagging.
- To change the level of difficulty, assign fewer or more taggers.
- Add equipment; for example, when tagged, an individual must perform 10 wall passes with a basketball.

Tennis Ball Frenzy

Equipment

- One tennis ball (or beanbag or ball of wadded-up paper) for each student
- One container for each team (large enough to hold all of the team's balls)
- One cone for each team to designate the starting point
- Stopwatch

Description

Divide each team into two smaller teams to create a total of 8 to 10 teams for the activity. Provide each team with one cone to designate as the starting point. Because this activity can be considered competitive, have each team's members do a team break and cheer before starting and give each other high fives when the activity is over. Place the containers at one end of the gym with each container positioned directly across from its designated team, which sits by its cone at the other end of the gym. On your signal, each team works to get all of its balls into its container five times in a row as quickly as it can; the activity is timed. At least two of the balls must be tossed by one team member and caught by a different team member.

Each time a team gets all of its balls into its container, its members high-five each other and yell "done!" After all team members have high-fived, they quickly remove the balls and run back and around their starting cone. Next, they transport the balls to the container in a different manner (e.g., skip instead of run). Upon finishing this second round, they again yell "done!" and high-five each other. This process continues for three more rounds, with each round involving a different manner of moving the balls to the container.

After the fifth round, tell each team its time. Try this warm-up again the next day and see if the teams can beat their previous day's time. You can also add the times of the two smaller groups from each larger team to give the full team its total time. Make sure that all teams high-five and congratulate the other teams. On the third day, you can have teams try once again to beat their previous best; or you can have the teams compete.

May I Assist You?

Equipment

Any good gym music

Description

After students have been greeted and are sitting with their teams, explain that when the music starts they are to jog throughout the gym while avoiding collisions. Then, when you give the signal (generally after about 30 seconds of jogging), each student pairs up with someone nearby and plays rock-paper-scissors. The loser sits down while the winner continues moving throughout the space but in a different manner than before. Throughout this process, the music never stops playing.

While the winners continue moving, they can free someone who is sitting by offering a hand and helping him or her get back into the game; they cannot, however, help the same person they played in rock-paper-scissors. When a person is freed, he or she begins moving again but in a different way than before. Soon, everyone who was sitting will be freed, and all students will be moving in a manner different from before. On your next signal, the students once again pair up and play rock-paper-scissors (each with a new person). As before, the loser sits down while the winner finds another way to move. Soon enough, all of those who are sitting are helped up by a friend and find their own new way to move. This process continues as long as you like.

Variations

- After a student is helped up to rejoin the game, he or she must say thank you and the name of the person who provided the help.
- Instead of having students play rock-paper-scissors, give each student a die and have players roll to see who wins. (The person with the smaller number sits.)

Gift Collection

Equipment

- Large mixture of small items (at least five per student), such as beanbags, tennis balls, balls of crumpled paper, shuttlecocks
- Bucket or box for each team

Description

This is a great warm-up that can be used either outdoors or in the gym. Each team gathers in a circle and does a team break and cheer before getting under way. To prepare for the activity itself, scatter the gifts (i.e., beanbags, tennis balls) around the activity space and have each team gather around its bucket or box. The teams' boxes should be in a straight line and be at least 20 to 30 yards away from the scattered equipment. On your signal, all members of each team run to collect one gift each (i.e., one of the small items) and return to put it in the team's bucket. Each child should have at least five chances to bring back a gift, so you need a lot of gifts (e.g., at least 150 for a class of 30 students)! Team members continue retrieving gifts until all have been collected. Only one gift per person can be brought back at a time. Of course, if the gifts are located farther from the buckets, students get more of a workout.

After all of the gifts have been collected and placed in a bucket or box, students can each take a few gifts and run out to scatter them for the next attempt or for the next class. If you want your students to get a super workout, write the name of an activity on some of the gifts. After all gifts have been collected, students pick out five of the gifts from their bucket and do the activity written on each of the gifts. Alternatively, you can assign a monetary value to each type of gift (e.g., 10 cents for a ball of crumpled paper, 25 cents for a shuttlecock, 50 cents for a tennis ball). After all gifts have been collected, each team calculates the total worth of its gifts. Another option is to write character-education focus words (in chapter 3) on some of the gifts. After all gifts have been collected, each team shares with the class one of its words and defines the word.

Variations

- Time the activity. See if a team can beat their time or set a new gift collection record.
- Have the students move in a different manner each time they collect a gift (e.g., run, gallop, skip).

Stations

Equipment

- Good gym music for movement
- Any equipment you want for your stations

Description

When students come into the gym and report to their teams, point out the stations that you have set up at various spots in the gym. Each station should require a movement or task to be completed by each team. For instance, station 1 might require a total of 200 rope-jump repetitions divided among the team members; the team must figure out how many jumps that involves per person. Similarly, station 2 might require a total of 200 jumping jacks, station 3 might require 100 push-ups, and so on. Accommodations can be made as needed. For example, if one team member cannot do the indicated number of individual repetitions, another member can pick up the slack. Or, if one student has trouble with rope jumping, he or she can jump over a rope placed on the floor. In other words, each team member contributes what he or she can at a given station.

Decide how many stations to use and how many repetitions to require for each activity, based on what is right for your class. Teams can begin the activity when you start the music, and they can change stations when you signal them to do so. Equipment needs depend on your choice of activities. Each team should execute a team break or cheer before starting the activity and give a round of high fives after completing all of the stations.

Variation

Each team stays together for a lap of jogging between stations.

Get a Grip

Equipment

- Rope for each team (15 to 20 ft., or 4.5 to 6 m)
- Good gym music for movement

Description

After students have received their greetings and reported to their teams, give each team a length of rope. Instruct the students to each stand up and find a place along the length of the rope. Every student should hold the rope with one hand, and all should face in the same direction. When the music starts, students move in a manner indicated by you (e.g., hopping, skipping, galloping, running) while continuing to hold the rope. When the music stops, students make a shape with the rope. You can call out a geometric shape (e.g., square, triangle) or a letter or number. When the music starts, the students again hold the rope and travel through the gym using a new method of locomotion.

Variations

- Instead of making a shape when the music stops, students perform 20 repetitions of a certain exercise.
- When the music stops, the students drop the rope to the floor and make the shape on the floor.
- Call out a math problem for students to answer by making the correct numerical shape with the rope. For example, if you say, "5 plus 5 minus 8," the students use the rope to make the numeral 2.
- Instead of making a shape with the rope, students make a word with their bodies—without letting go of the rope.

Circuits

Adapted, by permission, from D.R. Glover and L.A. Anderson, 2003, *Character education: 43 fitness activities for community building* (Champaign, IL: Human Kinetics), 68-70.

Equipment

- One circuit card per team (example content detailed in the Description section)
- Four mats
- Six to eight gym scooters
- Good movement music

Description

This is one of our favorite warm-ups, and we suggest continually changing the activities on the circuit cards. After students have reported to their team huddles, call each captain to come forward to receive his or her team's circuit warm-up sheet. Each team must complete all activities on its sheet together—that is, as a team. In other words, no one is allowed to run ahead and finish early, and you should emphasize this point to the class. Consider playing popular

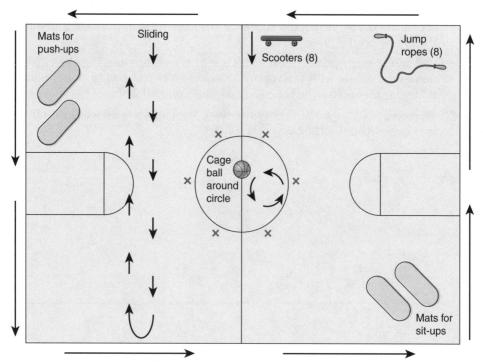

Jogging path around perimeter of gym

music while the students are warming up. We like using the music as a signal. You might say, "Once the music starts, you may begin," or, "When the music stops, please freeze."

Each team's card includes an identical set of circuit exercises, but the order varies in such a way that two teams are not at the same circuit at once. Here is a sample:

Circuit Warm-Up for Team 1

- Touch eight separate lines on the floor with your right hand.
- Complete 50 jump-rope repetitions.
- Jog five laps around the perimeter of the gym.
- Report to the push-up mats and try to do 20 push-ups; if you get tired, you may use your knees.
- Touch four separate walls with your left hand.
- Report to the sit-up mats and try to do 20 sit-ups.
- Slide the width of the gym eight times.
- Report to the gym scooters and lie on your tummy on a scooter. Scoot half of the width of the basketball court six times; use your arms to propel the scooter.
- Sing two verses of a song to your teacher.
- Report to the cage ball and roll it around the circle 10 times. (Teammates form a circle with their backs to the inside of the circle. Roll the ball around the outside of the circle.)

Team Problem Solving

Equipment

- Ten plastic hoops
- Favorite gym music

Description

After the greeting, students sit with their teams. The hoops are positioned on the floor throughout the gym. When the music starts, students jog anywhere they choose in the gym; encourage them not to jog as a team but to venture out on their own. While they are moving, change the way in which they move by calling out different locomotor movements.

Instruct the students not to touch anyone while they do the next section of the activity. Stop the music and call out a math problem (obtained from the classroom teacher) that is consistent with the students' age and grade level. Students then gather in their teams around one of the hoops, figure out the answer to the math problem, and put that many students inside the hoop. When all teams are finished, call out the correct answer; teams that got it right share high fives. Restart the music to signal students to begin moving around the gym again. This process continues for as many math problems as you want to do.

The first challenge faced by students in this warm-up is deciding how to come together, and at which hoop. The second challenge involves determining the correct answer, and the third challenge involves deciding who should get into the hoop. For example, if the correct answer is five and the team has seven members, which five team members get into the hoop?

Variations

- Make it a race and keep score. Award five points to the first team with the correct number of students in its hoop, three points to the second team, and one point to the third team.
- Put paper and a pencil inside each hoop and have students answer history or geography problems. Students must write the correct answer, put it in the hoop, and yell "done!" Scoring is the same as for the math warm-up.
- Require the teams to go to a different hoop each time the music stops.
- Give the math problem after the teams have gathered at their hoops and require them to solve the problem with paper and pencil. This variation can help students who have difficulty in math be a part of a successful conclusion to a math problem. Students with advance math skills will be good examples of how fun math can be and, with the teacher's encouragement, help mentor the students who have difficulty with math.

Bridges

Equipment

Favorite gym music

Description

After the teams have performed a greeting and are sitting in their circles, explain the activity. As with all warm-ups, each team should do a team break and cheer. Then, when the music starts, each team stays together and jogs anywhere around the gym or field. When the music stops, each teammate makes a bridge with her or his body (hands and knees); the bridges must be high enough for a student to crawl under. Each member of the team takes a turn going under all of his or her teammates' bridges.

When the music restarts, the teams once again jog together in open space. As before, when the music stops, each student makes a bridge, but this time each student takes a turn going both under and over his or her teammates' bridges. When going over, students must attempt a vault by placing their hands on the bridge (student's back); they may not simply jump or leap over. The pattern, then, is over, under, over, under, and so on.

When everyone on each team has completed the over–under pattern, the music restarts and students once again jog together with their teams. When the music stops this time, all team members lie facedown on the ground, and each teammate takes a turn leaping over all of the flat bridges. The music restarts, and the team jogs again. When the music stops again, each student stands straight and tall while his or her teammates take turns running around the standing figures (either weaving between or completing a circle around the standing teammates).

When the warm-up is finished, each team's members should high-five each other and get ready for the next activity. Routinely encourage high fives after each warm-up activity.

Variations

- Change the way in which the teams move each time the music starts.
- Change the way in which the bridges are positioned (e.g., scattered, in a line).
- Change the distance between bridges.
- Change the configuration parameters of individual bridges—for example, standing with feet spread (go under), lying flat (leap over), bending over on all fours (crawl through), holding hands with a partner at waist height with arms extended (run and duck under).

Playing Cards for Fitness

Equipment

- Two decks of playing cards
- Two sets of 14 numbered bases or cones to serve as stations
- One activity card per station indicating both an activity and the desired number of repetitions
- Necessary implements (e.g., jump ropes, basketballs) for your chosen activities
- Favorite gym music

Description

Number both sets of stations 1 through 14 so that each station corresponds with the number of a playing card (including 11 for jack, 12 for queen, 13 for king, and 14 for ace). Scatter the stations around the activity space and place an activity card under each station. After students have been greeted, explain the activity, and prompt the teams to each do their team break and cheer. When you start the music, one member of each team jogs over to you, picks a playing card from one of the decks, and takes it back to the team.

Once a team gets its card, its members jog together around the gym until they find the corresponding station number (again, jack through ace correspond to 11 through 14, respectively). Then, they look under the base or cone and perform the activity indicated on the activity card. Once the activity is complete, the student who drew the playing card gives it to a teammate, who jogs over to you, gives it back, and gets another card. This process continues until all team members have drawn a card. Once the team implements the last card, team members exchange high fives and get ready for the next activity.

Variations

- Students do the number of repetitions corresponding to the number of the playing card drawn (10 reps for all face cards).
- Vary the activity stations each time you use this warm-up.
- Add a station for the joker card that allows each team to choose its activity.
- Set up enough stations that each team member can draw two cards, thus giving each team a chance to do a wider variety of activities.

- Designate a certain card (e.g., queen, king) as special and set up a special activity at the corresponding station (e.g., healthy treat to eat).
- Here are some suggestions for station activities:

  Exercises of all kinds

  Basketball passing or shooting

  Floor hockey passing

  Football passing

  Tossing and catching a tennis ball or beanbag

  Scootering through and around a series of cones using only one's arms for propulsion

Team Egg Exercise

Equipment

- One plastic hoop
- One paper bag for each team
- One plastic egg for each student
- Small strips of paper, each labeled with an exercise name and number of repetitions and placed inside an egg
- Favorite peppy gym music

Description

Place each team's paper bag in a designated part of the gym—for example, in each corner (and, if you have more teams than corners, at the middle of the end line). Place the plastic hoop at the center of the gym (inside the center circle if there is one); then place the exercise eggs inside the hoop.

After the teams engage in a team break and cheer, start the music, which cues students to have one member of each team run to the center of the gym, pick up an egg, and bring it back to the team. The team opens the egg and performs the activity indicated on the strip of paper. The first runner then puts the egg in the team's paper bag, whereupon the second runner goes to the hoop and brings back another egg indicating the team's next activity. This process continues until all teammates have retrieved an egg.

This activity is not a race; stress to the students that they should perform the activity together rather than racing. When the activity is completed, encourage high fives with everyone on their team.

Variations

- Use your imagination when choosing exercises to put into the eggs. Include activities that support skills from the unit you are currently studying; for instance, if you are in the midst of a basketball unit, include activities that promote basketball skills.
- Place multiple hoops in the middle, one for each team; each team's eggs can contain the same exercises, but different groups will retrieve them in different orders.
- Time the activity, so that the next time the activity is done, you can challenge the teams to beat their previous time.
- Require each team member to move to the center hoop in a different manner than those used by his or her teammates.
- Require each team to jog a lap together before getting another egg.

Five-Minute Run

Equipment

- Lively gym music
- Four cones

Description

Place one cone in each corner of the gym, about 10 feet (3 m) from the wall; these cones outline the running track for the activity. After students have been greeted and are gathered in their teams, explain to them the importance of cardiorespiratory fitness and the role that jogging or running can play in the development of good health. (This lesson can be done with a classroom unit on heart health.) Talk also about selected character-education focus words (e.g., *perseverance*, *diligence*, *pride*) and explain how these qualities help us do our best work even when we are tired.

To prepare students for the activity itself, explain that when the music starts they should begin jogging around the track. They do not have to stay with their teams and can run at whatever pace they feel comfortable with. At the same time, encourage them to do the best they can; if they need to slow down to a walk at some point, they should start running again once they have recovered. Explain that if they pace their run effectively, they may be able to run for the whole five minutes without stopping. After everyone is done jogging, revisit the focus words addressed earlier and ask the students if and how they displayed those qualities in this activity.

Variation

Increase the run time to six minutes and then to seven minutes.

Follow the Yellow Brick Road

Adapted, by permission, from D.R. Glover and L.A. Anderson, 2003, *Character education: 43 fitness activities for community building* (Champaign, IL: Human Kinetics), 72-73.

Equipment

- Two chairs
- Two tables
- Nine cones
- Six small hurdles (3 by 6 in., or 7.5 to 15 cm)
- Music of your choice (optional)

Description

This is our favorite warm-up, and it can be used in many ways. You can have students do this warm-up after they report to their teams or as soon as they enter the gym (once they know that the "road" is up). The road follows the perimeter of the gym, which should have a cone in each corner, set far enough away from a wall to allow students to pass safely between the cone and the wall. With music playing (optional), students walk along the road. After one or two laps, give a signal for students to switch to a new method of locomotion—for example, skipping, sliding, galloping, jogging, running faster, running with a partner, or

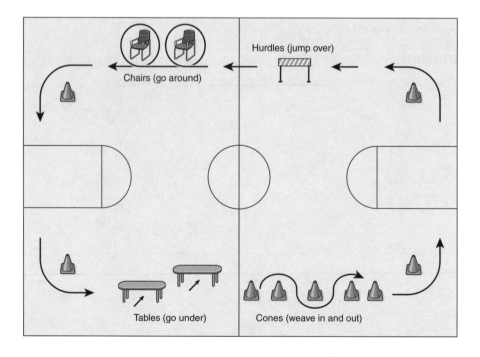

running with one's team. To make this warm-up even more fun, place obstacles in the road, such as the following:

- Hurdles to jump over
- Tables to go under
- Cones to weave around
- Chairs to go around

Variations

- Place a sign in each corner indicating a certain locomotor movement; students use that method of movement to get to the next corner.
- Integrate a game of Feed Tag. At one corner, place a stuffed animal (Tag). At another corner, place items to serve as Tag's food (e.g., tennis balls, beanbags, balls of crumpled paper). Students walk the first lap, grab an item of food, and then follow the road to feed Tag. When they get to Tag's corner, they place the food in Tag's box and continue along the road. Younger students are quite imaginative and love to pretend that they are feeding a hungry animal! To keep the activity fresh, allow students to bring in favorite stuffed animals to feed.
- Change the method of locomotion after each lap.

Shadow Dancing

Adapted, by permission, from D.R. Glover and L.A. Anderson, 2003, *Character education: 43 fitness activities for community building* (Champaign, IL: Human Kinetics), 85-86.

Equipment

Two to four overhead projectors (or as many as you can get if you want a bigger shadow area)

Description

Arrange the overhead projectors so that one entire wall is lit up enough to show the students' shadows. Arrange dimes (or draw dots) on the glass plates of the overhead projectors so that the shadows show up at different heights on the wall. Students (and their shadows) can then jump over, duck under, jump and touch, or crawl under the shadow obstacles. Let students run one at a time along the entire length of the wall while maneuvering their shadows through the obstacle course. You can also allow five or six students to try the course at once if they are sufficiently spaced out.

Variations

- Have students try the obstacle course while dribbling a ball or tossing a ball over a shadow and trying to catch it.
- Have students try the obstacle course while connected to a teammate.
- Have all six teammates go through the course while holding hands.

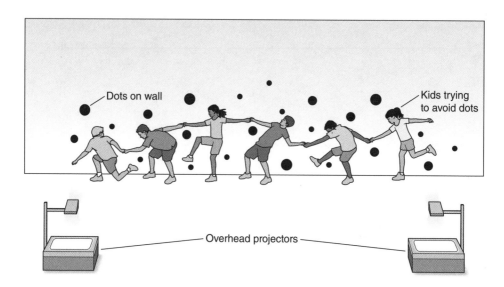

- Project a different obstacle course onto each of the gym's four walls and allow the teams to rotate among the courses.

- Have teammates start simultaneously at opposite ends of the obstacle course. Since they are traveling toward each other, they will have to make planning decisions when they get to the middle.

- Take away all shadows (i.e., dimes or dots) to leave a big, blank, illuminated wall. Position one team in the light, facing the wall, and then bring a pencil slowly down from the top of the light. Tell the students that Darth Vader is here with his shadow saber: "Do not let Darth Vader tap you with the saber!" The students duck under the saber shadow and run to the opposite side of the wall. Students love this activity.

- Position one team sideways in the light so that the team members can turn their heads and see how their shadows move. When students stand sideways, they can see their limb movements better than when they face the wall. Now call out sport moves (e.g., volleyball bump pass, basketball jump shot, baseball pitch); use as many different skills as you can think of. Students enjoy watching their shadows as they perform these skills. You can also point a projector at each wall and designate each "shadow maker" light for a different sport. Then do the activity again but this time with students directly facing their shadows.

- Record a video of students' shadows as they execute their sport moves; then show it to the class.

- Challenge students' reaction times with a shadow object. Have students face the wall on which the shadows appear while you quickly move an object on the overhead. Students try to touch or tap it.

Disc Math

Equipment

- Twenty to thirty flying discs (or poly spots), each with a number (1-20) and an exercise written on one side (okay to have the same number on two discs)
- One plastic hoop for each team and one for the center of the gym
- Lively gym music
- Twenty to fifty numbered index cards (numbered from 1 to 20; okay to have several cards with the same number)

Description

Place one hoop at the center of the gym and put the index cards facedown inside of it. Place the other hoops around the outside of the gym and assign one to each team; the teams gather around their respective hoops and await your instructions. Scatter the numbered discs around the gym with the number and exercise name facing down. Give the students their instructions, prompt the teams to perform a team break, and then start the music to begin the activity. One person from each team runs to the center hoop, picks up an index card with a number on it, and brings it back to the team.

The team must now find discs with numbers that add up to the number indicated on the index card. To do so, team members must first figure out what number combinations can work. (There are many possibilities!) Once they have decided how to solve the addition problem, one teammate runs to a disc and turns it over. If it has a number that the team wants, the team member takes the disc to the team and the members perform the exercise or activity indicated on it; when they have finished, the next two teammates run out to another disc or spot and turn it over. If, on the other hand, the disc has a number that the team does *not* want, the team member leaves it in place and returns to the team.

The next person then runs out, and the process continues until the problem is solved. When the team is finished collecting discs, the team members place the correct numbered discs faceup inside their hoop so that you can check their work. When all teams have solved their respective problems, or when time runs out, the warm-up is over. Students then return the discs and numbered index cards and prepare for the next round.

Note: Each team may want to plan two ways to solve its problem in case the team members cannot find one of the needed numbers. (Some teams may need the same number.) If a team tries all available discs and cannot find the needed numbers, it can replace its original index card. You can also have some blank cards available and write another number if needed.

Variations

- Time the activity. Teams like to do several rounds of this activity, and it is extra motivation if they can set a time record for solving a math problem.
- Use subtraction or multiplication problems or, for middle school or high school students, higher-level math problems. (This may call for more numbered discs.)
- When the correct disc is found, it must be tossed back to the team and caught by a team member before they can use the disc to solve the problem.

Add On

Adapted, by permission, from D.R. Glover, 2006, *40 Years in the gym: Favorite physical education activities* (Champaign, IL; Human Kinetics), 11.

Equipment

Music (perhaps students' choice to motivate them to complete the activity)

Description

Students report to the gym and sit with their teams. When you give a signal (we prefer music), they jog with their teams around the perimeter of the gym. At some point, you give another signal (e.g., turning down the music, clapping hands, hitting a drum), whereupon each team stops and performs 10 repetitions of an exercise chosen and led by a team member. When finished, the team returns to jogging around the gym.

When you give the next signal, a different member of each team leads 10 repetitions of a new exercise, as well as 5 repetitions of the first exercise. After another jogging stint, you give another signal, and a third member of each team leads 10 repetitions of a new exercise, as well as 5 repetitions of both the second and first exercises. This sequence continues until everyone on each team has led an exercise. Whew! This can be a tough warm-up if you require at least one lap of jogging before each new exercise.

Variations

- Change the way in which the teams move around the gym after each exercise session.
- To make the warm-up easier, have teams do only 1 repetition of each previous exercise in each round.
- To make the warm-up harder, have teams do 10 repetitions of each previous exercise.
- Add equipment, such as basketballs, footballs, or scarves.
- Allow each team to break up if a member needs to walk, but make sure that fitter students encourage any who do need to walk.
- Provide a list of activities on a large chart and have students complete the exercises in that order.
- Students can add on getting together outside of school time and doing a civic project together. This approach could be tough in large school districts as it may be difficult to arrange transportation for a larger area to cover, but smaller districts with students living closer together can do it. If a team accomplishes a civic task, write it up for recognition in the school announcements and community news publications.

Seven Jumps

Adapted, by permission, from D.R. Glover and L.A. Anderson, 2003, *Character education: 43 fitness activities for community building* (Champaign, IL: Human Kinetics), 87-88.

Equipment

Music: "Seven Jumps" song

Description

After students been greeted and have gathered with their teams, tell them that they will stay together as a team during this warm-up. The song for this activity, titled "Seven Jumps," has been around for ages. It features a lively folk-dance rhythm interrupted by a series of beeps. When the music is playing, students can move around the gym together as a team in whatever way the music leads them to move. When the beeps sound, they do the following: lie on stomach (first beep), lie on back (second beep), and kneel (third beep). Each time the music restarts, they once again move around the gym. As the beeps continue, continue the rotation of stomach, back, and knees throughout the song. This is a great warm-up!

Variations

- Try doing an exercise (e.g., push-ups, sit-ups) for each beep.
- Add equipment for use during the jogging portion (e.g., basketball, hockey stick and puck).

Poly-Spot Alphabet

Equipment

- Seventy-eight poly spots, each marked with a letter—three poly spots for each letter in the alphabet. If the teacher would like to make the activity a bit more difficult, use each letter only twice. (This would equal 52 poly spots.)
- Favorite gym music
- Paper and pencil for each team

Description

Divide each team into two equal groups. (This description applies to a class of 30.) Scatter the poly spots around the entire gym area. Start the music and direct the students to skip around the gym. When you clap your hands, students change the way in which they are moving (speed, type of locomotor movement, or both). Each new movement should be performed for at least 30 seconds before the next change. Do at least five claps to prompt the students to make at least five changes.

When you stop the music, each student stands on a poly spot. When all students are in position, yell "Scrabble!" to prompt each team to gather in a predetermined area with its poly spots. Teams then have five minutes to spell as many words as they can using the letters shown on their poly spots. The words must be spelled out on paper and given to you at the end of the five-minute period. Letters can be used as many times as needed to make as many words as possible. Each team appoints a writer, who listens to all spelling ideas as the team races to generate words. When you have reviewed all of the words, declare the winner for that round. Students then scatter their poly spots around the gym and get ready for another game.

Rules

1. Only one poly spot can be brought back by each team member.
2. If two students reach a poly spot at the same time, they must resolve the tie by deciding who touched it first. If that doesn't work, they must bring the spot to you to have the question decided by a coin toss; the loser of the toss returns to his or her team without a spot. This approach encourages students to quickly find another spot rather than taking a chance on a coin toss.
3. The five-minute period for making words begins *not* when a team gets together but when you yell "Scrabble!" This approach forces students to quickly find their teammates and start working efficiently in order to make the most of the available spelling time.

Variations

- Allow each team to use each of its letters only once per word in making words.
- Require each team to make a three-letter word, a four-letter word, and a five-letter word.
- If a team can make a word that the other teams cannot define, the teacher may award a prize or recognition of some kind to reward such literary genius.
- Require each group to spell at least one word related to character education.

One, Two, Three O'clock Rock

Note: This activity is also a character-education fitness game. Therefore, you may want to use it as a warm-up or as a game after teaching character-related concepts.

Equipment

- One homemade clock for each team that is decorated with eight character-education focus words instead of the usual numbers spaced around the clock face; each clock sits on a poly spot
- Thirty-two index cards, each bearing an inspirational saying (four copies of each set of eight sayings), as well as the name of an activity and the number of the repetitions to perform
- Eight to ten footballs
- Eight to ten basketballs
- Eight to ten floor hockey sticks and pucks
- Favorite gym music

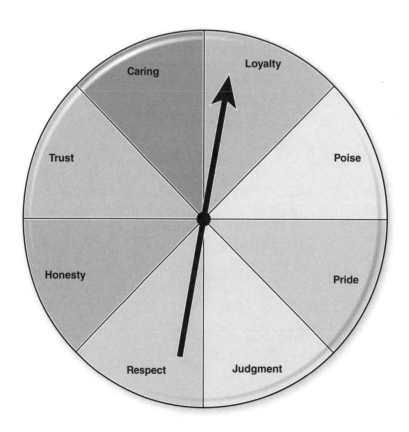

Description

Spread the clocks around the perimeter of the gym (one or two clocks—depending on the number of clocks used—on each side of the gym and one clock at each end of the gym). Spread the index cards facedown around the perimeter of the gym. When the music starts, students move wherever they would like inside the basketball court. Whenever you give a signal (e.g., whistle, clap), students change the way in which they are moving. When you stop the music, students find their teammates and decide which clock to gather around. Once there, someone spins the clock dial to indicate a focus word, and the team then moves together throughout the gym to find the card with the appropriate saying for the focus word. Table 2.1 shows sample focus words and sayings.

Table 2.1 Sample Focus Words and Sayings

Focus words	Sayings
Respect: feeling of honor or esteem for something or someone	During competition, show respect for your opponents, your teammates, and the officials. If you understand that everyone is doing her or his best, then show respect for their efforts. (20 rope jumps by each team member)
Honesty: truthfulness and trustworthiness (*not* lying, stealing, or cheating)	George Washington, the first U.S. president, said that the best title a person can possess is that of being honest. (10 push-ups by each team member)
Trust: confidence or firm belief in the honesty or dependability of someone or something	Trust in your future. If you prepare and work hard, you can achieve great things. (2 laps of jogging as a team)
Judgment: decision reached after careful consideration of evidence; ability to choose wisely	Use your best judgment and consider what you think you can do and what you cannot do. Remember your abilities and judgment experience will grow as you get older. Be honest with yourself and always do what is right. (20 total layups by the team)
Pride: sense of one's dignity or worth	Always do your best in school and life. Give your best effort; if you do not, you cheat yourself and others. Take pride in yourself. (20 sit-ups by each team member, working in pairs to hold each other's feet)
Poise: dignity and possession (or control) of one's own behavior and composure	Your response to events shows whether you have poise. Sometimes it is very hard to keep your poise or composure when you feel angry or upset; however, you can do it. (100 basketball passes, organized as the team chooses)
Loyalty: faithfulness to a person, country, idea, or type of conduct	If you are part of a team, school, community, or family, be faithful to your fellow members. Surround yourself with people you can count on—and make sure they can count on you. (20 floor-hockey passes with a teammate)
Caring: concern for others; inclination to look after others or contribute to their welfare	The world could use more caring people. It is noble to be concerned about the feelings of others. (20 football passes with a teammate to work on your spiral)

If they turn up a card that does not match the focus word, they leave the card in place and keep looking; the correct card's saying must contain the focus word (or a form of it). Once they find a match, they take the card back to their clock and put it under the poly spot. Next, still working as a team, they perform the activity indicated on the card for the specified number of repetitions. Then, they spin the dial and repeat the process; if the dial lands on a word they have already had, they keep spinning until a new word is indicated. This process continues until all eight focus words have been matched with the appropriate saying and the indicated activities have been performed.

Winter Sports

Equipment

Favorite gym music (perhaps seasonal)

Description

After students have been greeted and have joined their teams, explain that each team will move together in the gym area while following the lead of one team member. Then, when you stop the music and call out a winter activity, individually each team member will interpret and act out that activity. After 15 to 30 seconds, the music restarts, and the team agrees on a new leader and once again moves around the gym together. When the music stops again, you call out another winter activity. This process continues until everyone is warmed up; students should then exchange high fives.

Variations

Here are some suggested winter warm-ups:

- Figure skating
- Hockey
- Slalom skiing
- Throwing and dodging snowballs
- Speed skating
- Snowboarding moguls
- Snowshoeing
- Luge

And here are some warm-up ideas for summer:

- Water skiing
- Tennis
- Beach volleyball
- Kite flying
- Whitewater canoeing
- Swimming (three different strokes)
- Badminton
- Bicycle riding

Individual Team Warm-Up

Allow each team one day to select and lead the class in warm-ups; alternatively, allow each team to select its own warm-up for the day. For this activity to work, team members must reach consensus, which of course means that each student must take things in stride if his or her idea is not chosen. This approach also warrants a few reminders from you about being proactive by discussing how to handle potential problems before starting the warm-up.

SUMMARY

Creating a community of learners provides the foundation for effective teaching and learning. You may be passionate about the subject you teach, plan relevant and interesting activities, and deliver fascinating information—but none of this matters if students feel that they are not valued contributors or lack the needed support and encouragement to learn. This is especially true in physical education. Some of our most vulnerable students, the millions of obese children—students we desperately need to reach—deserve to learn in a safe environment where they feel accepted, supported, and valued. In order to start making a dent in the many disturbing health statistics we hear reported, we need to prioritize establishing a caring community of learners in our efforts to live active, healthy lives.

Strategies for Building Character

Children are 25 percent of the population but 100 percent of the future. If we wish to renew society, we must raise up a generation of children who have strong moral character. And if we wish to do that, we have two responsibilities: first, to model good character in our own lives, and second, to intentionally foster character development in our young.

Thomas Lickona, Character Matters (2004)

Character education is a growing educational initiative that supports students' social, emotional, and ethical development. The best way of teaching character is to provide students with opportunities to apply the concepts in real-life situations, and many such opportunities exist in physical education. Indeed, the majority of character traits we hope to instill in our students and athletes are addressed by helping them learn to be supportive teammates and respectful competitors.

Character education and emotional intelligence go hand in hand. The pillars of character education are traits such as trustworthiness, caring, respectfulness, responsibility, fairness, empathy, and good citizenship. Emotional intelligence, in turn, involves being aware of how emotions drive one's own behavior and the behavior of others. Our reactions to those emotions, whether positive or negative, determine how emotionally intelligent we are. For example, do we respond to negative situations with patience and optimism, or do we respond with anger and frustration?

The connection between emotional intelligence and character education lies in teaching students to be aware of their emotions and to respond in constructive ways. By developing the positive character traits of self-control, perseverance, patience, and compassion, students become equipped with the skills necessary to win with dignity and lose with pride. By developing traits such as optimism and self-awareness, they recognize that mistakes allow for opportunities to learn and grow. And by developing acceptance, compassion, and tolerance, they develop the skills needed to act as supportive teammates and respectful competitors. In these ways and more, physical education and sport offer a wonderful platform for creatively integrating these skills in a way that promotes healthy living—physically, socially, and emotionally.

This chapter covers the following character-building tools and terms:

- Focus words
- Reflection scenarios
- Video clips
- Inspirational sayings
- Songs
- Storytelling

FOCUS WORDS

Working with focus words, such as *integrity, pride,* and *perseverance,* allows students to construct meanings for terms and concepts that are essential to developing good character. Sample focus words representing positive character traits can be found in the book's web resource for this chapter. The resource also provides discussion prompts to deepen understanding and allow students to connect the words to their own lives.

Highlight selected focus words in class discussion and post them in the gym. It is very powerful to fill the gym walls with posters made by students representing the meanings and examples they generated. Seeing their work on the walls helps students feel empowered and develop a sense of ownership of their learning.

Of course, you cannot conduct long discussions in every class period, since physical education is an activity-based class. You can, however, introduce a new focus word either weekly or bimonthly, then discuss it with the class, and this approach goes a long way toward building young people of character. If you feel that you cannot take the time for discussion in physical education class, perhaps it can

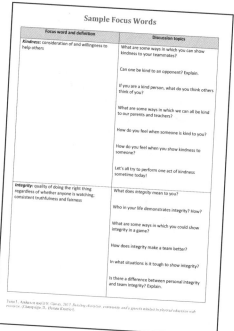

Sample Focus Words

Focus word and definition	Discussion topics
Kindness: consideration of and willingness to help others	What are some ways in which you can show kindness to your teammates?
	Can one be kind to an opponent? Explain.
	If you are a kind person, what do you think others think of you?
	What are some ways in which we can all be kind to our parents and teachers?
	How do you feel when someone is kind to you?
	How do you feel when you show kindness to someone?
	Let's all try to perform one act of kindness sometime today!
Integrity: quality of doing the right thing regardless of whether anyone is watching; consistent truthfulness and fairness	What does integrity mean to you?
	Who in your life demonstrates integrity? How?
	What are some ways in which you could show integrity in a game?
	How does integrity make a team better?
	In what situations is it tough to show integrity?
	Is there a difference between personal integrity and team integrity? Explain.

From L. Anderson and D.R. Glover, 2017, *Building character, community, and a growth mindset in physical education web resource.* (Champaign, IL: Human Kinetics).

be done in the regular education classroom. Teachers are always looking for ways to connect disciplines, and this is a great opportunity to do just that. It works best if, every week or two, the whole school focuses on the same word, which can be discussed, modeled, and reflected on in every classroom. Focus words also fit perfectly with the morning meetings that often take place in regular education settings.

Video Clips

Well-chosen video clips can provide students with powerful visuals and real-life examples of the character traits you are trying to teach. Search the web for useful video material from sources such as Values.com (from the Foundation for a Better Life), "On the Road With Steve Hartman" (a recurring segment on the *CBS Evening News*), and the *ABC News* "America Strong" feature. Many of the people featured in these videos are children, which helps strengthen the students' connections. The clips are often only about a minute long, yet they present meaningful stories demonstrating positive character traits. Therefore, they enable students to deepen their understanding by seeing what the concept looks like, feels like, and sounds like. These videos also tend to elicit emotion, and research indicates that connecting learning with emotion helps students retain content.

After showing a video clip, allow students to brainstorm the meaning of the selected focus word based on what they saw in the video. Then proceed to the focus word discussion topics, which are provided in the web resource. Of course, many younger students will have no idea what a word such as *integrity* means, but these videos will help them create relevant meanings. Consider the following progression:

> Teacher: "This week, we are going to learn all about the word *integrity*. We are going to watch a one-minute video with two boys demonstrating what *integrity* means. Their actions will provide a very good hint as to what integrity is all about."

Show the video.

> Teacher: "Based on what the boys did in the video, what do you think might be the meaning of *integrity*?"

Possible answers include the following:

- Helping people
- Making good choices
- Doing the right thing
- Not stealing

Of course, all of these responses are correct.

This type of process can be used for each focus word. After students understand the meaning of the word, proceed to discussion questions.

Y-Charts

Another great way to teach valuable character traits is through the use of Y-charts. Although many of the meanings may be too abstract for younger students to use this technique, it is well suited for middle school students and other students who already possess a basic understanding of what the chosen focus word means. See chapter 2 for details about how to use this technique to help students understand what a given focus concept looks like, feels like, and sounds like.

A related option is to show a short video clip and then assign one group of students to tell the class what integrity *looks* like. (Possible responses include the following: "It looks like people helping others." "It looks like happy people." "It looks like people cleaning up the earth.") Another group can be responsible for telling the class what integrity *feels* like. ("You feel happy." "You feel relieved that you did the right thing." "You feel calm.") And a third group can be responsible for telling the class what integrity *sounds* like. ("Can I help you?" "Let's do the right thing." "Thank you for helping me put the cones away.") Then allow each group a chance to share its results with the class. Once students have a good understanding of the word, the class is ready for discussion questions.

Whole-Class Discussion

A more traditional approach to facilitating students' understanding involves presenting the word to the whole class and then asking students for definitions. You could either ask students to raise a hand if they would like to share or task each team with presenting an answer to the rest of the class. If you take this approach, give students plenty of room to think and struggle in order to come up with a definition; in other words, don't be too quick to give them the answer! You can also ask for specific examples of how the concept is demonstrated by people in their lives.

After students have given their definitions in one manner or another, read them the dictionary definition, which is provided in the "Focus Words Discussion" web resource file. Next, follow up with the discussion questions provided (also in the web resource file).

Team Discussion

Before students conduct a team discussion, always reflect on what good teamwork and good team discussion look like and sound like. In addition, briefly review with students the role of the captain and the rest of the team during team discussions.

When ready, present the word to the class, whereupon each team, led by its team captain, discusses what the meaning of the word might be. Give teams one or two minutes to brainstorm, then ask them to share the definitions they have constructed. Provide them with the dictionary definition, then have the team captains facilitate their team's discussion by asking the questions provided for each focus word in the web resource file. If you don't have time to go over all of the discussion questions, then prompt the class to address one question per day or class period. Another way to address all of the questions efficiently is to give each team a different discussion question, then have the team captains summarize their discussion results for the class.

Athlete-Led Discussion

To increase the understanding and importance of these concepts periodically bring in high school student-athletes to facilitate discussions. In fact, this approach provides a win-win experience for all involved. It offers a great leadership opportunity for the high school athletes, and younger students often look up to their older counterparts. You can also have student-athletes facilitate a separate discussion with each of the teams, which provides a great opportunity for older students to model how to lead a discussion. What a wonderful example it is when high schoolers add to the discussion by sharing personal experiences related to the focus word!

End-of-Class Reflection

Reflection plays a critical role in learning and reinforcing good habits; therefore, you should always make time to reflect at the end of each class period. For example, if the focus word is *integrity*, you might ask students, "What acts of integrity did you notice during our game today?" The process requires as little as 30 seconds and can be done while students wait in line before being dismissed or during their cool-down. Whatever the situation, the little time required for reflecting on desired behaviors goes a long way toward strengthening the understanding of the focus words and how they relate to life.

REFLECTION SCENARIOS

Reflection scenarios enable you to take a proactive approach to helping students handle conflict. By constructing ways to handle these scenarios, students are better prepared to positively work through difficult situations.

Give the class a quick reflection scenario that relates to the selected focus word. It is easy to create your own reflection scenarios to encompass whatever dilemma or situation your students may encounter. This approach can produce great discussions and teachable moments in your class.

Here are some tips for integrating reflection scenarios into your classroom:

- Use the same strategies suggested for presenting focus words.
- Give each team a copy of a given scenario to discuss. Ask students to identify at least two focus words that are relevant to the scenario.
- You can also let each team read the scenario and then generate questions to ask their classmates.
- Provide the teams with different scenarios to read and discuss, identify relevant focus words, and explain to the class why they chose those words.

The following discussion prompts are presented in the form of real-life situations that students can relate to using their own knowledge and experience. Each scenario description also indicates the relevant focus words.

Recognizing That Someone Needs Help

Kindness, initiative, integrity

On Fridays, the sophomores on the varsity soccer team are in charge of making sure that all equipment is gathered and put away. On one particular Friday, due to a special school event, Cate is the only sophomore who is able to attend practice. After practice, while the girls are packing up to head home for the weekend, Cate heads out to the field to start gathering the equipment. Lizzie, a senior on the team, anxiously starts walking to her car, ready to begin the weekend. When she looks back to say goodbye to her coach, she sees that Cate is on the field cleaning up all by herself. Lizzie sets down her bag, runs out to help Cate, and encourages the rest of the team to do the same. As a result, what could have taken 20 minutes for Cate to clean up alone takes only 5 minutes because her teammates pitched in to help.

Reflection Questions

- What are some character traits that describe Lizzie?
- How do you think Cate feels when Lizzie takes the initiative to help her without being asked?
- What do you imagine the rest of the team thinks of Lizzie when she sets down her bag and goes out to help?
- Does Lizzie teach the team a lesson? If so, what do you think it is?
- Would you have taken the time to help Cate? Why or why not?

Counting on a Friend for Help

Kindness, resourcefulness, integrity, reliability

Cora and Rachel have a big math test tomorrow. When Cora gets home, she realizes that she left her math book in her locker. She starts to panic but then realizes that Rachel probably remembered hers. She calls Rachel, explains what happened, and asks if she can borrow Rachel's book when she is finished studying. Rachel says, "Of course you can! Or how about I bring it over now and we can study together?" Instead of having to make excuses, Cora finds a way to get the job done. As a result, she feels relieved—and happy that she can count on her friend Rachel.

Reflection Questions

- Instead of making an excuse, what does Cora do?
- What are some character traits demonstrated in this story?
- How do you think Cora feels when Rachel offers to study with her?
- Do you think people know they can count on you? How do you feel about that?

- Do you think Cora would now be more open to helping others when they need it? Why?

Boy in Masai Village Creatively Saves His Father's Cattle

Initiative, resourcefulness, integrity, tolerance

Go to Ted.com and search for the TED Talks by Richard Turere titled "My Invention That Made Peace With the Lions." This is a great story about a boy and a dilemma. Play the seven-minute talk for your students, then ask the following questions.

Reflection Questions

- What is Richard's problem or dilemma?
- What are some of Richard's character traits?
- What do you think about the way in which Richard handles his problem?
- How do you think Richard feels when his invention keeps the lions away?
- How can you or your teammates show initiative when preparing for a game?
- Many people would have chosen to just kill the lions. How does Richard's plan demonstrate tolerance?
- If you participate in a sport but lack direction in the off-season, how could you take initiative and be resourceful to ensure that you continue to improve?

Stopping Bullies

Courage, initiative, integrity, kindness

This is Bobby's first day at a new school. As he walks to his locker, he sees some older students picking on a younger, smaller student—knocking his books down and threatening to lock him in a locker. Bobby doesn't like bullies, and his first thought is to tell the teacher right away, but his second thought is to avoid getting involved. Still, he feels that he must help the bullied student, so he walks over and says, "Please leave him alone." Bobby then helps the boy pick up his books and makes sure that he gets to class.

Reflection Questions

- What do you think about Bobby's actions? How might you have handled the situation?
- What are some character traits demonstrated by Bobby?
- Do bullies have a lot of courage? Why do they bully others?
- The next three questions do not need to be answered aloud; just think about the answers.
  - Have you ever bullied someone? How did it make you feel?
  - Have you ever been bullied? How did that make you feel?
  - What are some different types of bullying?

Taking a Risk

Courage, confidence

Carol decides to try out for the track team at her middle school. On the first day of practice, the coach demonstrates hurdling and asks if anyone would like to try being a hurdler. It looks like a tough sport, but Carol thinks that she might like to learn and feels confident about trying. She raises her hand. Four years later, as a senior in high school, Carol is the conference champion in the 100-meter hurdles.

Reflection Questions

- What are some character traits demonstrated by Carol?
- Why is it sometimes difficult to try something new?
- How does Carol demonstrate confidence and courage?
- How can a lack of confidence or courage hold us back?
- How do you think Carol feels after becoming so successful as a hurdler? How might her success affect her willingness to continue trying new things?

Camp Workout

Resourcefulness, initiative, discipline

Carlos has decided to go out for football in high school, and he feels excited about starting a workout program at the YMCA. After the first two weeks of the program, he is more excited than ever and also feels well prepared for the start of the season. Then, during the third week, Carlos' dad tells him that the family is leaving on a camping trip in two days. Carlos wants to go on the trip but does not want to miss his workout program. He knows there must be a way to solve this problem. After giving it some thought, he asks his dad to let him work out on the camping trip for two hours per day, and his dad agrees.

When they arrive at the campsite, Carlos collects items from the forest that he can use to stay in shape. He does his squats with a log. Instead of bench presses, he does chest flies with two pieces of firewood. He also finds a tree branch big enough to hold him for pull-ups, does sit-ups while holding a sizable rock on his chest, and finds a hill on which to do incline sprints. Afterward his workout, instead of taking a nice warm shower at the Y, he swims in the lake next to the campsite. Carlos enjoys the camping trip and continues to get into great shape for football.

Reflection Questions

- What are some of Carlos' character traits?
- Have you ever faced a situation in which you had to figure out a clever way to work around a problem? Provide a short description.
- Would you have gone on the camping trip? How would you have handled the situation?
- How does Carlos demonstrate discipline and commitment?

Serving the Community

Citizenship, service, kindness, generosity, initiative

Maria's basketball coach tells the team that they will be doing some service learning projects during the season. Maria isn't thrilled about that and doesn't see the point. The first activity is to serve food at the local shelter for homeless people. Maria's first job is to serve plates of food to people at the tables. The people she serves are so friendly and appreciative of her efforts that she feels bad about not wanting to come in the first place. Afterward, Maria feels good about herself and how she helped others. She finds herself eager for the next project, which involves trick-or-treating for cans of food. Because of these experiences, Maria realizes that it is important and rewarding to serve the community. As a result, she plans to find ways to do so even after the season is over.

Reflection Questions

- What are some character traits demonstrated by Maria?
- How does Maria feel after serving her community?
- Is there a community project in which you enjoy participating?
- Why do you think Maria wants to continue serving her community?
- What are some other ways to be a good citizen?

Dirty Look

Forgiveness, integrity

Mark misses a critical free throw late in the Bears' first game; as a result, the Bears lose. Mark's teammate John gives him a dirty look and shakes his head. Mark, who felt bad enough already, gets angry with John for the dirty look. During the next week of practice, however, Mark realizes that he shouldn't stay mad at a teammate and that doing so only makes the team weaker. Therefore, he silently forgives John and decides to encourage and praise John whenever it is appropriate. In this way, he hopes to teach John that tearing down a teammate makes the team weak, but building up a teammate makes the team better.

Reflection Questions

- What are some character traits demonstrated by Mark? By John?
- Who would you rather have for a teammate—Mark or John? Why?
- Why is it hard to forgive someone who treats you badly?
- Do you agree with the way Mark handles the situation? Why or why not? What are some other things Mark could have done?
- Can you forgive yourself when you make a mistake?
- How do you think Mark feels when he finally decides to forgive John?

Get Out of My Way!

Patience, discipline

Matt always has to be first. He runs to get ahead in the lunch line; gets mad if the teacher doesn't call on him right away during discussions; and, on the baseball field, wants to be first at bat and first to pitch. In short, Matt generally gets very upset if things don't work out just the way he wants. One day, Matt is heading to gym—his favorite class—and wants to be there right away, but the student in front of him is walking very slowly. Matt calls him a name and says, "Get out of my way!" The physical education teacher hears Matt and makes him apologize to the other student. He also makes Matt sit on the sideline for half of the class period.

Reflection Questions

- What are some character traits of Matt?
- What happens to your body when you feel really impatient?
- What are some better ways in which Matt could handle his frustration?
- What are some fair ways in which students can decide who goes first?
- How can students handle a team member who acts like Matt?

Overwhelmed

Resilience, discipline, perseverance

Note: Invite a high school student to read this one, discuss his or her schedule, and share with your students ways in which he or she practices resilience.

Dave is swamped with schoolwork during the first semester of his senior year. He also plays on the school soccer team and holds down a part-time job stocking shelves at the local grocery store. Dave wants to spend more time with his friends, but there just doesn't seem to be any time to spare. He knows that next semester his class load will be lighter, and he isn't planning to participate in a winter sport. Even so, he feels tempted to switch to some easier classes in order to make his fall more manageable. Instead, he decides to prioritize his activities, make a schedule, and stick to it. It does indeed prove to be a long, hard semester, but Dave perseveres and gets through it. By creating a plan and working hard, he is able to get good grades, keep his job at the store, and stay on the soccer team.

Reflection Questions

- What are some of Dave's character traits?
- There are times in our lives when we feel overwhelmed by busy schedules and homework. How can we handle these situations?
- How do you think Dave prioritizes his schedule? What might he identify as most important? Why?
- How do you think Dave feels after completing a successful first semester?
- How does Dave demonstrate discipline?

Left Out

Pride, confidence

Alan is new at school and doesn't have many friends. He and his mom have moved four times already this year, so he has attended four schools. At each of the first three schools, by the time he started meeting people, he had to move again. At this point, he is beginning to hate school; it's hard always being the new guy and having no friends. As a result, Alan spends most of his time working by himself or sitting alone during free time. He tries to avoid gym class and recess because he always gets left out. He often tells the teacher that he doesn't feel well or that he just wants to stay in and get his work done. He feels embarrassed and uncomfortable and wishes that the other students would ask him to join them for school activities.

Reflection Questions

- What are some of Alan's character traits?
- Does Alan have pride in himself? Does he have pride in his school? Why or why not?
- What are some ways in which Alan might come to feel better about his school and himself?
- What are some ways in which Alan's new classmates could help him?
- How can you gain pride in your team? In your schoolwork? In your community?
- What does it mean to have pride in yourself? How do you gain that pride?

300 Miles

Diligence, pride, discipline, perseverance, motivation

Christina wants to make her school's varsity cross country team. She knows that in order to do so, she has to run a six-minute mile, but her best time during the previous year was 7:05. She decides to try to run at least 300 miles (483 km) during the summer in order to get into top shape. She sticks to her plan and logs 305 miles by the time cross country season begins. During the first week, the coach holds a time trial, and Christina makes the varsity team by running her personal-best mile time of 5:47.

Reflection Questions

- What are some of Christina's character traits?
- How do you think Christina feels after making the varsity team?
- How are your goals similar to Christina's?
- Would it have been easy for Christina to give up? Why?
- How do you think Christina's teammates feel about her, knowing how hard she has worked?

The Pencil Fairy

Generosity, kindness, initiative

LaQisha notices that three of the kids in her classroom do not have pencils and therefore always have to borrow one from the teacher or a classmate. She remembers that at home, in one of the cupboards, her mom has a collection of pens and pencils that she has gathered over the years. By now, it includes more than 50 items! She asks her mom if she can give some to her classmates who don't have any, and her mom says yes. The next day, LaQisha brings three pencils for each of her classmates in need.

Reflection Questions

- How does LaQisha show initiative?
- What are some character traits of LaQisha?
- Who in your life has similar character traits? Explain.
- How do you think LaQisha feels after she shares the pencils?
- Has anyone ever been generous to you? How did that make you to feel?
- When is it difficult to be generous? Why?

Making the Varsity Team

Motivation, initiative, pride, perseverance, discipline, resourcefulness

Jesse wants with all her heart to make the high school varsity basketball team. She did okay on the freshman team this year, but there are no guarantees that she'll make varsity next year. Just before summer break, the freshman coach meets with all the girls and tells each girl where she needs to improve: "You're a good ball handler," he tells Jesse, "and you play great defense, but you really need to improve your outside shooting."

Immediately, Jesse starts making a plan to improve. She decides to shoot 300 shots per day and finds out that the gym is open most days from four o'clock to six o'clock in the evening. As for days when the gym isn't available, she decides to use the basket in her driveway. She also recruits family members to rebound the ball, pass it to her, and keep track of her makes and misses. During the first part of June, Jesse makes 28 percent of her outside shots. She feels very motivated to improve and keeps practicing. By the middle of August, she is doing a lot better, making 40 percent. One day, she even makes 26 of 50 three-pointers! Jesse feels great about her improvement and now looks forward to the upcoming season.

Reflection Questions

- What are some of Jesse's character traits?
- In what situations have you been as motivated as Jesse?

- How does Jesse show initiative and discipline?
- How might motivation contribute to the success of a team?

Making Good Choices

Discipline, courage, integrity

Caleb's gym class is playing soccer when his friend Isaac rolls his ankle and falls to the floor in pain. Mr. Mars, the gym teacher, wants to carry him to the nurse's office but feels worried about leaving the class alone. He quickly tells the kids to sit down and remain seated while he steps out of the gym to take Isaac to the nurse. However, as soon as he leaves the gym, two girls stand up to get the soccer balls. Caleb politely asks them to sit back down. He feels bad about saying anything, but he knows that Mr. Mars would be upset. Three other kids also speak up and tell the girls to sit down. The girls end up sitting down just before Mr. Mars returns. He tells the class how proud he is of them for listening and demonstrating self-control.

Reflection Questions

- What are some character traits demonstrated by Caleb?
- Integrity and discipline involve doing the right thing even when nobody is watching. Are these traits demonstrated by the students in Mr. Mars' class? How so, or how not?
- Think about the power of peer pressure. Now, consider this question: Would you have made the same decision as Caleb?

Power Play

Tolerance, integrity, discipline, pride

Two hockey teams, the Hornets and the Saints, are playing for the conference championship. The game is tied 2-2 going into the third period, and things are starting to get rough. With only four minutes remaining, two players begin to fight, and the ref calls a penalty on both players. Chen, the Saints player, disagrees with the call and argues with the ref. As a result, an additional penalty is called on the Saints, which gives the Hornets a power play. With just 20 seconds left in the power play, the Hornets score, and they go on to win the game and the championship.

Reflection Questions

- What focus words relate to this scenario?
- How do Chen's actions affect his team?
- Why is it sometimes hard to be tolerant of calls made by game officials?
- If a team member disagrees with a call during a game, how should it be handled?

We Can Do It!

Cheerfulness, optimism

John-Paul always seems to take a positive attitude. When his football team loses the first game of the season, the team acts like the world is going to end, but John-Paul looks at it differently. "Come on, guys," he says. "We could have won that game. We just made a few mistakes. Let's get fired up for next week." The coach notices John-Paul's approach and says to his assistant coach, "That kid never gets down—I hope his attitude rubs off on more of the team."

Reflection Questions

- What are some of John-Paul's character traits?
- How might his attitude affect the team?
- Can cheerfulness be spread? Is it hard to be cheerful all the time? Why or why not?
- Do you know a truly cheerful person? How does that person lead you to feel?
- Do you think John-Paul feels sad after the loss? Is it okay to feel sad? Is it okay to bring others down with you when you feel down?

Let's Get Fired Up!

Enthusiasm, discipline, optimism

Sanyu loves volleyball and works hard year-round to improve her skills. In the past year, she played on the varsity high school team during the fall, played in AAU during the spring, and attended a volleyball camp in the summer. As a result, her skills improved rapidly. Now, she can hardly wait for her senior season to begin. When it does, Sanyu is not only one of the top players on the team but also the team's biggest cheerleader. Her enthusiasm for the sport is contagious. She constantly supports her teammates with high fives and encouraging words. Her team wins the conference championship, and many people feel that Sanyu deserves the MVP award not only for her skill but also for her enthusiasm.

Reflection Questions

- How can enthusiasm affect a team?
- Do you have to be enthusiastic about something in order to be good at it? Why or why not?
- How are motivation and enthusiasm similar?
- How did Sanyu act as a leader both on and off the court?
- Can you accomplish great things without enthusiasm? Why or why not?

Adversity Makes Us Stronger

Perseverance, forgiveness, optimism

Harun is very excited about gym class today because the subject is team building. The teacher has said that she will put out some tough challenges, and Harun is determined that his team will succeed. On the first challenge, however, Harun's team fails over and over. Frustration begins to set in, and Harun gets angry at his teammates and accuses them of not giving 100 percent. It's obvious that a breakdown has occurred, and Harun wants to quit.

In contrast, Harun's teammate George recognizes that there is no way the team is going to succeed if everyone is angry and frustrated at each other. He suggests that the team move away from the challenge and talk about how they can work through the adversity they are experiencing. He encourages his teammates and tells them that he feels confident they can solve the challenge if they work together. Harun realizes that he was wrong and apologizes for being negative. The team members make a commitment to each other that they are going to be positive and supportive. Although it takes them a bit longer than expected, the team is ecstatic when they finally succeed at one of the most difficult challenges.

Reflection Questions

- What are some traits demonstrated by the team as a whole?
- What would happen if George didn't step up and encourage the team members to talk about their frustration?
- How do you think the team members would feel if they decided to quit?
- We experience failures every day, often several times per day. Why is it so easy to get frustrated? How can one work through frustration positively?
- An old saying tells us that adversity makes us stronger. How might this be true?

Conference Player of the Year

Discipline, perseverance, integrity

Bao has had a very successful junior year in lacrosse; however, despite putting up some of the most impressive stats in the conference, she is not named to the all-conference team. When she talks to the coach about it, he explains that the likely reason is her negative attitude. During the season, she often complained to the refs about calls and yelled inappropriate things at the opposing team. Upon hearing her coach's analysis, Bao feels devastated but responds by committing herself to exercising discipline both on and off the field during her senior year. She comes up with strategies for using self-control when she disagrees with a ref or feels frustrated. Her coach is so impressed with her self-improvements during summer camp that he names her as team captain. Bao enjoys a great senior year, not only in terms of statistics but also in her teamwork and good sporting behavior. At the end of the season, she is named as the All-Conference Player of the Year.

Reflection Questions

- What focus words does Bao demonstrate? How?
- How is self-discipline different from being disciplined by one's parents or teachers?
- How can self-discipline in individual players contribute to a team's success?
- How do you discipline yourself to do well in school?
- What similarities exist between the meanings of *discipline* and *self-control*?

Tough Loss

Integrity, discipline, kindness

The Saints are playing for the regional championship in high school basketball. If they win, they advance to the state tournament; if they lose, they are done for the year. It's a great game that comes down to the final seconds. With the Saints down by one and one second left, Jadyn, the Saints' point guard, is fouled while taking a jump shot. If he makes both free throws, he can give his team the win. The crowd goes wild as Jadyn calmly steps to the line. He misses the first shot but still has a chance to tie the game. The second shot rolls around the rim twice, then falls out. The Saints lose the game, and Jadyn falls to the floor in disappointment. One of his teammates, Jaquan, puts an arm around Jadyn and does everything he can to help him feel better. Another teammate, Kaleem, walks by him and gives him a very angry look.

Reflection Questions

- What do you think Jadyn feels when he misses both free throws?
- How do his teammates likely feel?
- How does Jaquan show discipline by not reacting to his own disappointment but instead showing concern for Jadyn?
- Who would you rather have on your team—Jaquan or Kaleem? Why?

Reaching Out

Kindness, integrity

Every day in physical education, the students greet each other with a handshake or high five. Some students, however, avoid certain classmates because they don't want to shake their hand. In particular, they always avoid Jeff. Two other students, Alexa and Dennis, recognize how Jeff is being treated, and they make a point to give him a high five.

Reflection Questions

- What is the purpose of greeting classmates?
- How do you think Jeff feels when certain students in the class avoid him?
- What are some character traits demonstrated by Alexa and Dennis?
- How would you handle it if you saw kids intentionally being unkind to a classmate or teammate?

Good and Not-So-Good Teammates

Integrity, kindness

Jabbar and Jontay are both very good athletes; in fact, they are considered two of the best in the school. Jontay is also a very good teammate, but Jabbar is not. Jontay never brags about his skills, and he regularly encourages others. Jabbar, on the other hand, acts like he is better than everyone else. He frequently puts down his teammates when they make a mistake, and he rarely says anything positive. One day, the teacher allows two students to pick teams. Jontay is picked well before Jabbar, and Jabbar can't figure out why he is picked last when he is such a good athlete.

Reflection Questions

- Who would you rather have on your team—Jontay or Jabbar? Why?
- Why do people sometimes act cocky?
- How would you handle having a guy like Jabbar on your team?

Good Athlete, Bad Teammate

Integrity, pride, discipline, tolerance

Brenda is an excellent athlete and very competitive. Her goal is to win—no matter what. She often gets very upset and yells at teammates who aren't as athletic as she is. One day, while playing basketball, her best friend, Kim, tries to pass Brenda the ball and accidentally passes it to the wrong team. Brenda yells at Kim in front of the whole class. Kim remains calm, focuses on encouraging the rest of the team, and goes out of her way to encourage and praise Brenda when she does something to help the team.

Reflection Questions

- How do you think Brenda's words and actions affect the team?
- What are some things that teammates might say or do to help Brenda be a better teammate?
- Who would you rather have on your team—Brenda or Kim? Why?

VIDEO CLIPS

Many short but powerful videos are available for use in character education. Often only a minute or two long, these clips elicit students' emotions, which is known to strengthen learning. All of the clips suggested in this section can be found by searching common websites. They show true stories of people (often children) modeling strong character. Showing a video clip to introduce a new focus word (i.e., character trait) gives students a chance to construct the meaning of the term. If facilitated effectively, these real-life stories often generate meaningful conversations with students.

Many of the clips suggested here are from Values.com, the *ABC News* segment "America Strong," or the *CBS Evening News* segment "On the Road." If you simply type the video's title into an online search engine, you should find the correct video. The following listings include a brief description of each clip, its approximate length, and the focus words it demonstrates.

Famous Failures With Michael Jordan Video (2:59)

Perseverance, pride, resilience, courage, motivation, discipline

This video highlights some of the most successful people in the world and how they failed many times before succeeding. It is appropriate for middle school and high school students; the words *suicide* and *drugs* are used in one example.

Maybe It's My Fault—Nike Commercial Featuring Michael Jordan (1:02)

Perseverance, pride, resilience, courage, motivation, discipline

This video talks about how Michael Jordan made his success look easy and explores how much hard work it actually took for him to succeed.

Failure—Nike Commercial Featuring Michael Jordan (0:33)

Perseverance, pride, resilience, courage, motivation, discipline

This video focuses on Michael Jordan's failures, which he credits for his success.

Blind Pole Vaulter Soars Past the Odds—"America Strong" Feature (2:31)

Perseverance, pride, resilience, courage, motivation, discipline

High school athlete Charlotte Brown broke a school record on the pole vault. The video addresses how she overcame blindness by learning how to pole-vault and accomplish her goals.

Duracell Commercial Featuring Derrick Coleman (1:04)

Perseverance, pride, resilience, courage, motivation, discipline

This video portrays Derrick Coleman, an NFL player who is deaf. The clip shows that Coleman experienced adversity while growing up but chose to persevere until he accomplished his dreams.

Derrick Coleman Hopes to Inspire Kids to Overcome Obstacles—*Good Morning America* Feature (4:25)

Perseverance, pride, resilience, courage, motivation, discipline, confidence, optimism

This clip highlights Derrick Coleman's story in greater detail. Here, he talks about his book, *No Excuses,* and demonstrates how he faced the obstacles of hearing impairment and bullying to become a stronger person.

Never Give Up: The Homeless Teen Who Is Graduating the Head of the Class—"America Strong" Feature (2:10)

Perseverance, pride, resilience, courage, motivation, discipline, confidence

This clip portrays a high school senior who has been homeless throughout his life. He does not let his situation become an excuse. Indeed, he ends up graduating high school as valedictorian of his class.

Attitude More Important Than Altitude for High School Football Player—*CBS Evening News* "On the Road" Feature (2:32)

Perseverance, pride, resilience, courage, motivation, discipline, confidence, tolerance, compassion

This clip highlights a high school football player who is 4 feet (1.2 m) tall. This young man does not give up, and his teammates rally around him in support.

Football Star Shows You Can't Judge a Book by Its Cover—*CBS Evening News* "On the Road" Feature (3:19)

Perseverance, pride, resilience, courage, motivation, discipline

This clip tells the story of a Georgia football star joining a women's book club. Malcolm Mitchell grew up not knowing how to read. Instead of using that as an excuse, he was determined to learn.

A High School Basketball Miracle in Minnesota—*CBS Evening News* "On the Road" Feature (3:15)

Perseverance, pride, resilience, courage, motivation, discipline, teamwork

In this story, a high school girls basketball team experiences a four-year, 83-game losing streak. They finally break their streak despite a very difficult game situation.

Basketball Team With Little Fans Gets Support From Unlikely Source—*CBS Evening News* "On the Road" Feature (2:54)

Generosity, integrity, initiative, citizenship, service, character, tolerance, kindness

This clip focuses on a basketball team from a juvenile detention center that typically has no fan support. One day, however, the kindness of an opponent makes it possible for the team to play in front of a gym full of fans.

Homeless Pay for Haircuts With Hugs in Conn. Town—*CBS Evening News* "On the Road" Feature (2:24)

Generosity, integrity, tolerance, kindness, character, initiative, citizenship, service

One man demonstrates kindness and generosity by reaching out to homeless people. He cuts their hair for free, getting paid only in hugs.

Cafeteria—Values.com (1:00)

Kindness, initiative, integrity, courage, character

In this public service announcement, a high school girl is new at school and has no one to sit with at lunch. Another girl recognizes her situation and sits with her.

Middle School Football Players Execute Life-Changing Play—*CBS Evening News* "On the Road" Feature (3:41)

Kindness, tolerance, integrity, character, initiative

A middle school football team schemes a secret play that allows a boy with a learning disability to score a touchdown.

A Tribute to Lauren Hill—*CBS Evening News* "On the Road" Feature (2:56)

Kindness, integrity, courage, perseverance, resilience, pride

This clip shows the power of love and determination. Basketball player Lauren Hill had a dream to play in a college game. Despite her terminal brain tumor, her dream came true thanks to her team, the opposing team, and the community.

Disabled Basketball Player Is Given Help by Opposing Player to Score a Shot—*CBS Evening News* "On the Road" Feature (2:38)

Kindness, integrity, tolerance, character, pride

Due to an opponent's good sporting behavior, a boy with a learning disability scores a basket in the final seconds of the game, and the crowd goes wild.

Young Baseball Fan's Act of Generosity—*ABC News* "Person of the Week" (2:10)

Kindness, integrity, character, generosity

During an Arizona Diamondbacks baseball game, a boy nabs a foul ball. Despite his excitement, he gives the ball to a younger boy who is sad because he didn't get there first.

Kindness Boomerang—Life Vest Inside (5:44)

Kindness, integrity, tolerance, character

This video shows how one act of kindness can inspire many others. The resulting chain of simple acts, set to music, involves both children and adults.

The Motivational Video—Bamboo Tree (3:42), Found on YouTube

Patience, perseverance, resilience

How long does it take a bamboo tree to grow 90 feet (27 m)? This clip reminds us that it takes patience to accomplish great things. The clip is set to music with pictures and words scrolling on the screen, so it's best suited for students in upper elementary through high school.

Man Inspires Hundreds to Spread Kindness—*CBS Evening News* "On the Road" Feature (3:39)

Citizenship, service, initiative, kindness, integrity, character

A man with ALS gives students $50 to go out and make the world a better place. They find many ways to do so with the various service projects they create.

After Losing Parents, 6-Year-Old Embarks on Smile Mission—*CBS Evening News* "On the Road" Feature (2:54)

Kindness, cheerfulness, initiative

A young boy turns his sadness into happiness by spreading cheer to complete strangers. He deliberately targets people who are not smiling and hands them a small gift.

Reach—Values.com (0:30)

Integrity, kindness

This video is an excellent way to introduce integrity. It shows two boys approaching a beverage delivery truck. The door of the truck falls open, giving them the perfect opportunity to steal some pop. How do they respond?

Including Others—Values.com (1:00)

Integrity, initiative, tolerance, kindness

A boy shows initiative by giving up his soapbox-derby race car to a boy with a disability who otherwise would have been left out.

INSPIRATIONAL SAYINGS

Inspirational sayings can help students construct meanings and apply them to their own life situations. This particular activity can be done in 5 or 10 minutes; adapt the lesson length to meet the needs of your students and program. We recommend introducing one saying every week or two. For example, if a focus word is presented on Monday and a reflection scenario on Tuesday, why not use an inspirational saying on Wednesday? We recognize, however, that many students do not have daily physical education. Therefore, use your best judgment when planning how to use the concepts presented in this chapter.

The first time that students discuss an inspirational saying could be structured as a whole group activity again, with you modeling how the team captain should facilitate it within their team. The saying could be displayed on a wall or handed to students in writing as they walk in the door. The class could read it together, or a student might volunteer to read it aloud. For each saying, you can ask the following three general questions to facilitate discussion.

1. What does this saying mean?
2. Give specific examples of how it might relate to a situation in physical education or in your life.
3. Now that you understand this saying, how might it affect your actions or thoughts?

After you facilitate these discussions once or twice, students may be ready to take over the discussion within their teams. To use this approach, give the team captains the saying on a sheet of paper (for examples, see the web resource for this chapter). They can read it aloud, then ask the three general questions to facilitate discussion. In addition, rather than displaying store-bought posters, some teachers have invited students to create their own inspirational sayings to hang on the walls.

Sample Inspirational Sayings

We are what we repeatedly do. Excellence, then, is not an act but a habit.
–Aristotle, ancient Greek philosopher

Storms make oaks take deeper roots.
–Proverb

What lies behind us and what lies before us are tiny matters compared to what lies within us.
–Henry Haskins, stockbroker and originator of many great quotations

I am convinced life is 10 percent what happens to me and 90 percent how I react to it.
–Charles R. Swindoll, founder of Stonebriar Community Church in Frisco, Texas

You miss 100 percent of the shots you don't take.
–Wayne Gretzky, NHL hockey legend

An obstacle is often a stepping stone.
–William Prescott, Revolutionary War colonel

If we only did things that were easy, we wouldn't actually be learning anything. We'd just be practicing things we already knew.
–David Dockterman, education lecturer at Harvard University

Character is a diamond that scratches every other stone.
–Cyrus A. Bartol, 19th-century pastor of West Church in Boston

The master has failed more times than the beginner has even tried.

SONGS

Music can be a great teaching tool for character education. Provide the class with a copy of appropriate song lyrics to read together, stopping along the way to discuss certain phrases or meanings. Alternatively, students can use the lyrics to follow along while they listen to the song. Once students make meaning of the lyrics, play the songs during warm-ups or cool-downs. Discussing song lyrics instead of reflection scenarios or inspirational sayings on selected days not only offers a different routine but also reinforces the meanings of the focus words. You can then create a dance for the song to help students gain even more insight into the lyrics. Soon, the lyrics will become ingrained in students' minds, and they will start singing along.

Two songs with excellent character-education messages are John Legend's "True Colors" and Lee Ann Womack's "I Hope You Dance," and the web is full of many other appropriate songs featuring popular musicians. Students relate especially well to a song if it is performed by one of their favorite artists. If you do a web search for the phrase "positive, upbeat, inspirational songs you can dance to," you will get a useful list of songs (usually including the lyrics). Here are a few that we have found:

"Unwritten" by Natasha Bedingfield

"I Can See Clearly Now" by Jimmy Cliff

"Proud" (*The Biggest Loser* theme song)

"Larger Than Life" by Pinkzebra

"Gold" by Britt Nicole

"True to Myself" by Ziggy Marley

"Brave" by Sara Bareilles

"Crazy Dreams" by Carrie Underwood

"Get Back Up" by TobyMac

"Don't Give Up" by Bruno Mars and the Muppets

"What I Am" by Will.I.Am with the Muppets

In addition, here are some websites where you can find songs that teach character; some of the songs are available for free, whereas others must be purchased.

- Songsforteaching.com: Character Development Songs
- Songspun.com: Free Music for Character Education
- Redgrammer.com: Songs About Character
- HaveFunTeaching.com: Character Songs

STORYTELLING

Character education can also be conducted effectively through storytelling, and the sporting world provides many heroic stories about success in the face of obstacles. If stories are powerful moral tools—and they are—then physical educators have a full toolbox! As a result, it isn't too hard to find appropriate narratives and condense them for use with your class. Kids may also want to find a story on their own to share with the class; for example, many inspirational stories are always provided by the Olympics.

When you read a story to your students, read it with conviction and feeling, and have some discussion questions ready to enhance students' engagement with the story's significance. To add variety in facilitating an understanding of character-education traits, we recommend using stories at least once a month. Here are three examples of powerful stories to share with students.

Story 1: How Heavy Is This Glass of Water?

Do an online search for the story "How Heavy Is This Glass of Water?" Practice telling the story, and then present it to your class. Tell it with emotion, then ask your students some follow-up questions. Here are a few examples of good questions.

Discussion Questions

- How do stress and worry affect you?
- What can you do to get rid of stress and worry?
- What are some things that cause you to feel stress?

- Who can help you overcome worry?
- Do your team, or individual teammates, add to your stress? Or do they help you cope with it?

Story 2: It's My Town

Harry's family moves to a new town, and he begins attending eighth grade at a new middle school. Because he is shy and finds it difficult to make new friends, he is not happy about the move. For the first week, when he comes home from school, he just watches TV, does his homework, eats dinner, and then watches more TV. One day, before bedtime, his mom says, "Harry, why don't you come to the food bank with me on Saturday and help me stock the shelves?" Harry feels glad that his mom is willing to help out at the food bank, but it isn't his thing, and there's no way he wants to do it. Harry feels comfortable with his routine and doesn't want to disrupt his weekend TV viewing.

Another week goes by, and again Harry's mother asks if he would please come volunteer at the food bank: "Several young people are involved, Harry. You won't be the only kid there." Harry thinks about it, rolls his eyes, and says impatiently, "Okay, okay. If you still need someone to help, I'll come next week." Another week passes with more of the same old routine for Harry. On Friday, his mother says, "Harry, remember the food bank tomorrow. We have to be there by 9 a.m., so set your alarm for 8 a.m. We'll work until noon." Harry reluctantly agrees, telling his mother, "Okay, I'll try it this week, but please don't ask me to go again after tomorrow."

The next morning, Harry and his mom arrive at the food bank to find other families stocking shelves and bagging groceries for clients. The manager tells Harry that he'll be working with the other kids in the back room to unload a truck and stack the delivered food on the shelves. When they get to the back room, Harry sees two other boys working there. One, Javari, is African American; the other, Akio, is Asian. Immediately, Harry feels very nervous. He has never been around black kids much. He feels a bit afraid that he might get beat up; he has seen black kids on TV, and his perception of them is that they are mean. He also figures that the Asian kid probably knows karate and could beat him up. He thinks to himself, "This is my last Saturday. I'll keep my mouth shut, do my job, and hope I get out of here alive."

To Harry's surprise, both Javari and Akio come over and introduce themselves, thank him for coming, and show him how to unload and where to stack. The three boys talk and work all morning, and they find out a lot about each other. Harry finds out the other two boys are a lot like him—they like sports, and they like to go to movies. In fact, he has such a good time that quitting time seems to come too soon. All three boys decide to come again next Saturday.

Harry, Javari, and Akio end up working together for almost all of the remaining school year. They become good friends and do the kinds of things that good friends do outside of school. When the school year is over, they decide to join the local summer recreation soccer team, and this experience brings them even closer together. As a result, when they start high school in the fall, they already know someone other than the kids at their respective middle schools. Harry has developed a different outlook about kids of other races. He also feels less afraid to try new things; for example, he decides to go out for the ninth-grade soccer team. And all of this happens because, as the old saying goes, "Mother knows best!"

Discussion Questions

- What does Harry learn from his experience?
- How common is Harry's initial attitude toward people of a different race?
- How do you feel about trying new things? What might lead you to feel nervous about it?
- Is it normal to feel nervous about meeting new people or trying new things? What can hold us back in such situations?
- Why does Harry now feel more at home in his new school and community?

Story 3: Senior Leadership

Despite being only the seventh seed, the Bears defy all odds and make it to the section championship game, with a trip to the state tournament on the line. The accomplishment is especially meaningful to the seniors, given the team's heart-breaking loss in the section championship the year before. In fact, they have been highly motivated to avenge the loss.

Leigh, a sophomore, wasn't part of last year's team, but as the section championship game approaches, she knows how important it is, especially to her senior teammates. The goal of going to the state tournament was set by the team at the beginning of the year, and it has been a topic of conversation throughout the season. Now, with the big game just a week away, Leigh begins to feel uneasy. The typical nerves that she often felt before regular-season games start turning into worry and anxiety. She wants this win so much for the seniors, and she starts to put a lot of pressure on herself and feels worried about having a bad game.

On game day, Leigh tries to relax and think positively. During lunch period, however, the tension becomes too much as a parade of students and teachers approach to wish her luck. Although they have great intentions, the comments only contribute to her stress. Recognizing that something is wrong, the senior captain, Brenda, pulls Leigh aside to see if she can help. Leigh breaks down and shares how worried she is that she will ruin the seniors' chances of going to state.

Brenda responds thoughtfully, saying, "We're so lucky we made it this far. No one thought we could do it. We're in the section championship partly because of your hard work and dedication to the team. Let's just enjoy every minute of this experience and do our best tonight. Whatever happens, we need to realize that we had an awesome season, and we had a blast along the way."

After talking with Brenda about her fears, Leigh feels better. She still goes into the game nervous—but also fired up. The Bears end up beating the Knights, the number one seed in the section.

Discussion Questions

- What do you think Leigh learns from this experience?
- What role does Brenda play in resolving the situation?
- How important is it to have good leaders on a team?
- How can fear, worry, and anxiety affect an individual's or a team's ability to function?

ADDITIONAL WAYS TO TEACH CHARACTER

To be creative and add variety to your approach in teaching character-education concepts, consider using the following methods in addition to strategies already presented in this chapter.

- **Modeling:** As a teacher, you know that the best way to teach is through example. Show students that you care by encouraging and recognizing them on a daily basis. When addressing students, use their first name to help them feel accepted and connected; there is just something special about hearing one's first name used in a positive manner. Be as positive and encouraging as you can; yes, this can be difficult at times, but a smile on your face says a lot about your positive attitude.
- **Positive reinforcement:** Continually recognize and reinforce positive character traits when they are displayed by students. All it takes is a simple comment, such as, "Wendy, you demonstrated great integrity by being honest in our volleyball game today. I couldn't tell if the ball was in or out. When you called it against your team, you modeled what honesty is all about." You can also create a bulletin board in the gym with index cards showcasing specific behaviors by students that demonstrate strong character.
- **Mentorship:** Invite older physical education students to help kindergartners and first graders learn physical education content. You can refer to the older students as coaches and the younger ones as teammates. This approach benefits both groups. The younger students get individual attention, which helps them learn skills faster; they also see older role models who show them that helping is a good thing. At the same time, the older students get the satisfaction of watching the younger ones learn and improve from their efforts. Teaching and caring about someone's learning is a great way to develop empathy and friendship. In our own classes, we give older students the opportunity to teach younger students as a reward for teams that show positive character traits.
- **Encouragement:** Encourage students to join extracurricular programs. In addition, model fitness and activity by exercising and letting your students see you walk or shoot baskets during your free time. On occasion, you can also invite high school athletes to visit as a way to inspire and encourage younger kids to get involved.

- **Home connections:** Keep parents informed about the character-education activities you are doing. Ask for their help and give them follow-up ideas to implement at home. Also ask them to closely assess the coaching philosophy of any team in which their children take part outside of school. It is counterproductive to spend time on character education in school only to have it undermined by a win-at-all-costs philosophy in another setting.

SUMMARY

We cannot assume that students come to us with strong positive character traits. Nor can we resort to punishing students for demonstrating negative behaviors without teaching them a better way. Desired behaviors must be taught. If you integrate the concepts presented in this chapter into your lesson plans, you will notice a big difference in your students' individual behaviors, teamwork skills, and love for physical fitness. Be deliberate in teaching valuable character traits. Model strong character and consistently reflect and reinforce positive behavior. If you do these things, you are well on your way to building healthy individuals with strong moral character. No other discipline in school provides such an excellent platform for preparing students and athletes to lead successful, active, and healthy lives.

Character-Building Games and Activities

Play is often talked about as if it were a relief from serious learning. But, for children, play *is* serious learning. Play is really the work of childhood.

Fred Rogers, television host of the famous children's show
Mister Rogers' Neighborhood

Learning by doing is a powerful way to learn. Learning while doing *and* exercising is even better! To that end, this chapter presents games and creative activities to reinforce the character-building concepts introduced in previous chapters. Whether we refer to this approach as playing with purpose or using activities that teach, it engages students in group activities that build and reinforce strong moral character.

Previous chapters have introduced the power of teaching through an integrated approach. The most natural setting in which to do so—by modeling and embedding emotional intelligence and character education—is physical education. When you consistently take time to reflect and provide specific praise, students naturally develop stronger character traits.

The activities presented in this chapter reinforce the meaning of the character traits that should be deliberately taught. Students' understanding is strengthened by the repetition of seeing, hearing, and feeling the meanings of these traits in fun games and exercises. As always, be proactive in your approach and encourage students to identify problems that may occur in the activities you introduce. By prompting students to identify possible conflicts and proactively brainstorm solutions, you position them for success while integrating conflict resolution skills.

These games are meant to enhance your existing curriculum, and they can be used either in a concentrated character-education unit or periodically throughout the year. Most of them do need to be played after students engage with a few focus words and reflection scenarios in order to better understand and successfully complete the objective of the game. In addition, almost all of these games require you to prepare new pieces of equipment (e.g., index cards with character-education terms and definitions. If an activity requires equipment that is not included, you may use equipment provided for another activity that is also in the web resource. Finally, as with all games in your curriculum, have students start these games with a team break and cheer and finish with a high five and reflection (see chapter 2).

Help Me Find My Character

Equipment

- One index card per student labeled with a character trait (e.g., for 26 students, 26 character-education focus words, each written on a separate index card)
- Large chart listing all of the chosen focus words (examples of which are included in the web resource for this activity) and posted where all the students can see it

Description

Have students work together using masking tape to attach focus-word cards to their backs (one per student); clothespins will also work. Each student should *not* see the word attached to his or her own back. On your signal, students begin trying to find out their respective words by asking each other questions. (You may choose to save this game for later in the year, after you have discussed many of the words.) Students can, of course, see the words posted on the chart, which gives them some idea of questions to ask.

Students may not simply ask what their word is, nor may they wiggle around this restriction by asking something like, "Is _____ my word?" Instead, they must ask questions to help them figure out what the word is, such as the following: "I had a hard time getting an A in math. I had to study every night." Or, "I found a ten dollar bill and turned it in at the office." Students being asked the question can only answer yes or no. When all students have figured out their words, they sit in a circle and try to articulate a definition for each word. You can then have students exchange words and do another round.

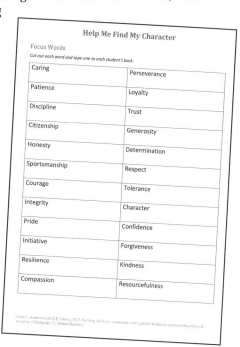

Variations

- To make the game much easier, use only a few words and make multiple cards.
- Require that each time a student asks a question, he or she must jog a lap before asking another.
- Time the activity and see how long it takes the class to get all of the words.

Matchmaker

Equipment

- Cone or base for each student
- Peppy music
- Sport equipment: four basketballs and one goal; two footballs; four floor hockey sticks and two pucks; two volleyballs
- Four jump ropes
- Fifteen index cards with a character-education focus word on one side and a number on the other side (indicating the number of reps to perform of the exercise indicated on the matching definition card)
- Fifteen index cards with a definition on one side (matching a character-education word) and an activity on the opposite side (e.g., layups, push-ups)

Matchmaker Game
Answer Key

Courtesy 40	Polite behavior / Jumping jacks
Punctuality 20	Promptness; tendency to be on time / Layups
Responsibility 20	Ability to taking care of oneself and others or to carry out a task carefully and thoroughly / Layups
Citizenship 20	Respectful devotion to one's school, community, or country; following the laws and duties of a citizen / Football passes
Kindness 20	Consideration of others and willingness to help others / Football passes
Resourcefulness 20	Cleverness, creativity, imagination, or inventiveness; ability to find ways to meet difficult situations / Hockey passes
Sportsmanship 20	Ability to experience winning or losing without gloating or complaining / Hockey passes
Cleanliness 20	Habitual and careful neatness / Volleyball passes
Honesty 20	Disposition not to lie, steal, or cheat / Volleyball passes
Gratitude 40	Feeling of thankful appreciation / Rope jumps
Resilience 40	Ability to manage change and snap back to normal after misfortune / Rope jumps

From L. Anderson and D.N. Glover, 2017, Building character, community, and a healthy mindset in physical education and recreation (Champaign, IL: Human Kinetics).

Note: Use an equal amount of focus word cards and definition cards. By using 15 of each, there are enough cards for 30 students to participate. You will need to adjust the number of each type of card to accommodate the number of students who are participating in your class.

Description

Place the cones or bases randomly around the gym. Put each focus word under a cone and each matching definition under a base. Alternatively, if you have two colors of cones or bases, one color can hide the focus words and the other color can hide the definitions. Have each student stand next to a cone or base.

When the music starts, students jog around the gym while using their agility to weave around the cones and their classmates. When the music stops, each student goes to an empty cone or base and, on your signal, looks under it and picks up the focus word or definition. When the music restarts, students move around and try to find the student with the matching focus word or definition. Before the game is played, the class should discuss what to do if a student does not have a match. For example, if the student picked a focus word card but did not find that matching definition, the student could run to the teacher and attempt to provide a definition, then do the exercise the teacher gives.

Once two students have matched their cards, they check the answer key (held by you) to confirm the match. Next, they perform the activity indicated on the definition card for the number of reps indicated on the focus-word card. When they have finished, the partners do a "walk-and-talk" around the gym and discuss whether they have seen examples of the focus word in school, at home, or on a sport team. Do not allow students to complete the same focus word–definition match more than once. When all pairs have finished, they put the focus words and definitions back under the cones or bases, and the game begins again.

Variations

- Change the way in which students move each time a new game starts.
- Time the activity. How long is it before the first match is made? How long before all of the focus words and definitions are matched?
- Rather than placing the cones randomly, position them along the outside of the gym, leaving enough space between the cone and the wall to form a large running track.
- Have each pair of students read their focus word and definition to the class.

Curling for Character

Equipment

- Floor tape (enough to make two targets and three starting lines for each group of competitors)
- Three gym scooters per team, preferably a different color for each team
- Index cards with character-education focus words (six per target)
- Key that lists each focus word and its definition
- One poly spot per team

Description

Use floor tape to make two targets (each about 6 ft. or 2 m square) at one end of the gym floor. In each target square, place six focus-word index cards of your choice. At the opposite end of the gym, use the tape to make starting lines (three for each group of competitors)—one that is even with the free throw line, another between the free throw line and the half-court line, and the third at the half-court line. Place each team's poly spot at its first (farthest) starting line.

During play, two teams shoot (i.e., roll a scooter) at their assigned target. The object of the game is for each team to collect as many focus words as possible by pushing its scooter toward the target from behind one of the starting lines. If the scooter stops within the lines of the square, the team collects one focus word on the condition that the team members give the correct definition. To

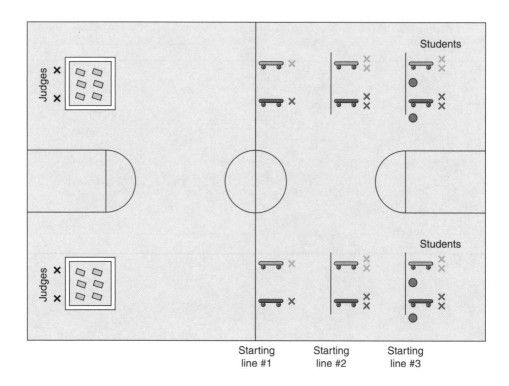

start the game, each team must decide who will roll the scooter and from which starting line. Each starting line must be used once in each round. When all three scooters from each team have been rolled, the teams collect the focus words they have earned and place them on their respective poly spots near their first starting lines.

Additional Rules

1. Each starting line must be used in each round. The team decides who will push from each line. The pusher at the half-court starting line pushes first, followed by the pusher at the next-distant line and then the one at the free throw line.

2. Three scooters are pushed by each team in each round. For example, if a team has six team members, then two of the scooters must be pushed by two team members; the remaining scooter can be pushed by one person.

3. One team member, designated as the judge, stands behind the target to assess whether a given scooter push scores a focus word; in order to count, a score must be confirmed by the judges from both teams. Each team appoints a new judge for each round.

4. When a team scores a focus word by landing its scooter within the lines of the target, the team members huddle up and decide on a definition for that word, then designate one team member to report the definition to you. The other team using that target must wait to start the next round. If you accept the definition, the scoring team keeps its focus word and places the card on its base at its first starting line. If the definition is not accepted, the team puts the focus word back on the target. The teams using that target then continue rolling.

Considerations

- As in traditional curling, one team's scooter can knock another team's scooter from the target.
- It is an advantage to go last, so the order of the teams should rotate each round.
- Do not allow excessive, vigorous pushes; they are not seen in the sport of curling and are not allowed in scooter curling.
- If you like, it is acceptable to have each student push from a different starting line in each round.
- In order to score, the scooter must stop completely within a square; it cannot touch any lines.
- Pushers are not allowed to approach the target at any time; only judges evaluate the scoring.
- This game is set up for 24 students; you can make more target squares and have fewer students at each target.
- For older students, move the starting lines farther from the targets.

Variations

- If it is not feasible to tape a target on the floor, use a mat divided into sections. Place two focus words in each section and have students toss beanbags rather than rolling scooters.
- Add numbers to the squares so that students can play to a certain number by accumulating points in each round. Teacher can decide the number needed to win.
- Instead of focus words, you can also use reflection scenarios (see chapter 3) or inspirational sayings (see the web resource for chapter 3).
- The scooters may roll truer if weight is added to them, so allow students to select a team member to sit on the scooter and push it to the target. The rider is not allowed to influence the direction of the scooter and must remain as still as possible. (**Safety note:** Warn the rider to lean forward during the initial push and to be careful not to fall backward off the scooter. You may want the rider to wear a helmet.)

Parachute Play

Equipment

- One parachute
- Six beach balls (8 to 12 in., or 20 to 30 cm) marked with character-education focus words (either write on the ball or on a piece of tape placed on the ball)

Description

After the students have been greeted and have participated in a warm-up, gather them around the parachute. They do not stay with their teams for this activity; rather, the teams mix as students find a space around the chute.

First chute activity: This activity is the team weave. On your signal, students raise their arms overhead while still grasping the chute. When you call out a team name, members of that team let go of the chute and run clockwise, weaving in and out of the students still holding the chute. When everyone on the team has returned to his or her original spot, call out another team name. This process continues until all teams have had a chance to weave around the chute. Now repeat the entire process in the opposite direction.

Second chute activity: Again, students should not be next to a teammate but intermixed with members of other teams around the chute. As in the first activity, all students raise their arms overhead and you call out a team name. The members of that team then try to exchange positions by each skipping to a teammate's empty space before the chute deflates. This process continues until all teams have had a turn. Now repeat the entire process but change the way in which students move when swapping positions.

Third chute activity: With students gathered around the chute and holding on to the rope edge or handles, put all of the beach balls on the chute, then assign one student from each team to serve as an outfielder. These students release their grip on the chute and move back two steps. On your signal, the other students begin shaking the chute vigorously, thus causing the balls to pop off of the chute. When the balls fly into the air, the outfielders try to catch them before they touch the floor. When a team's outfielder catches a ball, he or she puts it into a team area (designated before the game). If a ball hits the floor, it must be tossed back onto the chute by one of the outfielders. This process continues until all balls have been caught.

When all balls have been caught and stored, each team gathers around its outfielder and the balls that he or she has caught. If any team is without a ball, assign a team with multiple balls to lend one. Each team then picks one ball and discusses what the indicated character-education word means and whether they have seen an example of it in the gym. Did they perhaps even see it today? Prompt students to discuss how important the concept represented by the word is to the functioning of a team. What would happen if a team did not display this character trait? After their discussions, the members of each team exchange high fives.

Do You See My Reflection?

Equipment

- Four reflection scenarios (one for each team) from the web resource, each including in its description the focus word that it addresses
- Index cards that each bear one letter of one of the four focus words that match the chosen reflection scenarios (e.g., seven index cards which, together, spell the word *respect*)
- Index cards that each bear the definition of one of the four focus words
- One large chart that lists the four focus words and is posted on the wall for all teams to see
- One marker next to the chart
- One plastic hoop and one poly spot per team
- Four cones to mark the jogging path

Description

Scatter the teams around the outside of the gym in positions that put each team equally distant from the center. Each team is seated by its plastic hoop with its reflection scenario facedown in the center of the hoop. The index cards with letters are scattered in the center circle of the gym, and the definition cards are scattered around the gym under the four poly spots. On a signal from you, the chosen reader for each team turns over the reflection scenario and reads it to the team. The team now works to figure out which focus word is best described by the reflection scenario; remember, the word is used in the scenario description, and the team can also look at the large chart posted on the wall. Once the team chooses a word from the chart, it sends one member to the chart to place a check mark by the chosen word.

The team now begins collecting index cards marked with the letters of the selected focus word. It does so by having one member at a time run to the center of the gym, collect one letter, bring it back, and place it in the team's hoop. Once the letter is placed in the hoop, the team runs one lap around the gym, after which another team member runs for another let-

Do You See My Reflection?

Scenarios

Each focus word is embedded in its scenario.

Reflection Scenario 1

Becky is participating in a close game of basketball. During the game, she steps out of bounds while dribbling the ball. No one notices, but Becky values honesty, so she stops and gives the ball to the other team.

Reflection Scenario 2

Chen is new at his school. At his old school, he played on the soccer team, and he knows that he is a very good player; however, he does not know anyone at his new school yet. Knowing that he is shy, his parents encourage him to try out for the soccer team anyway. Chen builds up his courage, walks out to the soccer field after school, and asks the coach if he can play.

Reflection Scenario 3

During badminton class, Dick slams his racket into the floor after each missed shot. Jerry also misses some shots but decides that he has too much respect for his teacher and the equipment to wreck it.

Reflection Scenario 4

Joe and his buddy Bill are being teased by some students from another school. The students are making fun of Joe and Bill's school and teachers. Joe and Bill both feel loyalty toward their school and to each other. In fact, they know that they go to a great school, and they feel proud of it. They decide not to pay attention to the teasing.

Reflection Scenario 5

Pat and Tawana are watching TV after school when a news bulletin shows a fire at the local animal shelter. The girls decide to go to the shelter the next day to see if they can help. When they arrive, they find that the owners can use their help for many things. The girls love animals and enjoy being of service to the shelter staff.

Reflection Scenario 6

Keith loves his country and feels sad when he sees veterans on TV coming home after serving overseas. He notices that many of the veterans are injured and must spend time in the hospital. He gets some of his classmates to rake leaves and mow lawns for a week and then donate the money to a local charity that helps wounded warriors. The charity's representative, to whom Keith delivers the money, says that he is a patriot to help out the soldiers.

From L. Anderson and D.R. Glover, 2017, *Building character: community, and a growth mindset in physical education and cooperative.* (Champaign, IL: Human Kinetics).

ter of the chosen word. This process continues until the team's focus word is spelled out inside its hoop, whereupon the team travels, as a team, to find the correct definition. To do so, the team members jog together to each poly spot and read the definitions located there until they come upon the one they think is correct. When the correct definition is found, the team returns to its hoop, puts the definition next to the focus word, and sits down. When every team is done, each team reads its focus word and definition to the class.

The web resource for this activity includes six sample reflection scenarios and the matching focus words. You need only four if you have four student teams, but we have included six in case you would like to use more teams or simply would like a bigger selection of focus words. The six words each contain seven letters.

Variations

- Instead of running a lap after each letter, each member of the team does a different activity (e.g., makes a basket or dribbles a lap with a basketball). Substitute any activity or exercise you like.
- Use eight-letter focus words. Here are a few of the many possibilities: devotion, optimism, courtesy, civility, kindness, fairness, and patience.
- Do another round by having each team rotate to a new hoop.
- To force each team to search more diligently, put out additional poly spots with nothing under them.

Monster Mash

Equipment

- Twenty-four cones
- Four basketballs
- Twenty-four index cards (four sets of six), each bearing a negative word (e.g., poor sport, cheater, bully, selfish) plus a number and an activity
- Paper scraps, each bearing one letter of the word *character* (enough to spell the word four times)
- A large display chart listing positive character-education words
- Two plastic hoops for each team

Description

Tape a card indicating a negative word and an exercise onto each cone; tape each card lightly, so that it can easily be pulled off. For each team, position the cones in a straight line about 2 or 3 feet (0.5 to 1 m) apart and equidistant from the end line and the half-court line. Each team now has a line of six cones through which to dribble-weave, each with a different negative word and exercise. To begin the activity, teams line up at one end of the gym, behind the end line of the basketball court. Each team lines up behind the end line, next to their plastic hoop with a basketball, facing their row of cones.

On your signal, the first designated member of each team dribble-weaves through the cones and, on the return trip, picks up one of the cards listing a negative word and an activity from a cone in his or her line. Once the dribbler arrives back at the start, another team member dribbles out and retrieves another card in the same manner. Meanwhile, the rest of the team performs the exercise indicated on the card brought back by the first dribbler. This process continues until all of the cards have been collected and all of the exercises performed.

The team now has the right to collect the puzzle pieces (i.e., paper scraps, each bearing one letter of the word *character*), which you have placed in a plastic hoop positioned at the opposite end of the gym. Do not tell the teams the new word beforehand The first team member dribble-weaves through the cones, then dribbles to the hoop at the other end of the gym, brings back a letter, and places it in the team's home hoop. This action signals the next team member to dribble-weave through the cones and retrieve another letter in the word. This

Monster Mash

Negative Words

Make enough copies to use one set for each team. You will tape these to the bottom of cones.

Disrespect	Poor sportsmanship
20 jumping jacks	20 squat jumps (burpees)
Panic	Rude
20 sit-ups	30-second plank
Impatience	Dishonesty
1 lap of jogging as a team	10 push-ups

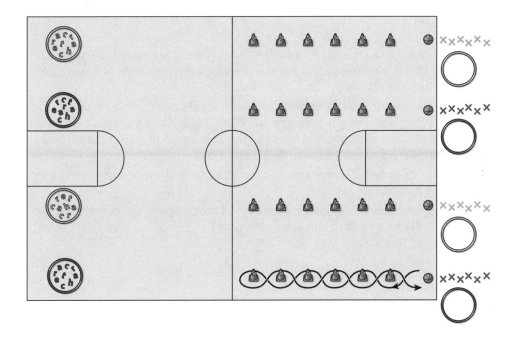

process continues until the team has gathered all letters in the word *character* and positioned them in the correct order in its home hoop. All team members should work together as needed to figure out what the word is and then spell it correctly.

Once all teams have finished this task, direct them as follows:

1. "Each team should now choose one negative word from the words they collected and then agree on its meaning and how it could affect a team. (Allow about two minutes for this discussion.) Once all teams are ready, each team will report its discussion results to the rest of the class." (Each team selects a spokesperson or two for this job.)

2. Now ask, "What does the word *character* mean? Each team has two minutes to come up with a definition." After two minutes have passed, have each team share its definition with the class, then give the class the definition: The combination of qualities and traits that makes one person or team different from another.

3. Now, to culminate, pose the following questions.

   • How well would your team function if the character of your team were based on your chosen negative word?

   • Who has witnessed or been part of a team that displayed any of the negative words? How did you feel when you saw or experienced that occurrence?

   • Review the chart of positive words, choose one positive character trait or quality that your team would like to possess, and be ready to tell us why.

Variations

- Divide each team into two smaller teams (you now have eight teams) and set out a line of four to six cones; with only three members per team, each student goes twice.
- Put an exercise and a number on each puzzle piece of the word *character*. When a puzzle piece comes back to a team, the team members must perform that exercise and the reps the number indicates. This approach provides quite a workout!
- Time the activity to see how fast teams can accomplish the task or set class records.
- Have students use a different method of movement (e.g., dribbling a soccer ball or using floor hockey equipment).

Basketball Dribble Battle

Equipment

- One basketball for each student (including one per team with an inspirational saying taped on it)
- Four colorful vests or pinnies

Description

Each team member has a basketball, and one member per team has a ball with an inspirational saying; in other words, if you have four teams, prepare four balls with a saying (different saying for each ball). Choose four defenders, one from each team, and have them put on a pinny or vest and line up at half-court. The rest of the students line up behind one end line of the gym. The object of the game is for the students to dribble their basketball to the other end of the gym and over the end line.

- All students can begin their dribbling journey once you start the music. They must get their basketball to the other end of the gym before you turn off the music.
- If a basketball gets knocked away by a defender, the dribbler must quickly retrieve the ball and begin again from that spot.
- Defenders try to disrupt the smooth flow of progress by each dribbler. They can do so by hitting the ball back toward the start line. Defenders may not catch or carry a ball; they can only hit or tap. They should do their best to slow the progress of all dribblers; they may not disrupt the same dribbler twice in a row.

Upon crossing the end line with the ball, each student finds his or her team, defenders included, and sits in a team circle to wait until all students finish. Teams then look at their inspirational sayings and discuss them. Allow about two minutes for the teams to figure out their meanings, then have each team select a member to report to the class about the team's discussion. When all teams have reported, select different defenders, have the teams exchange basketballs, and do the activity again. Don't worry about reusing the same saying— different teams will interpret it differently. However, if you would prefer to use a different set of inspirational sayings, you will need to prepare them ahead of time for the second round.

Variations

- Use one defender—this will make the dribble journey much easier and the activity will go much faster. If you use six defenders, it will be much harder for the dribblers to get to the other end of the gym without their ball being tapped.
- Have students use floor hockey equipment. (Put the inspirational sayings on the pucks.)
- Have students use a flying disc or a different kind of ball (e.g., foam, tennis, playground) and pass it to move down the court and over the end line.

Inspirational Race Game

Equipment

- Twenty-four index cards (four sets of six), each bearing an inspirational saying (such as those provided in the web resource) on one side and an exercise and a number of repetitions on the other side
- Favorite gym music

Description

All four teams line up behind one end line of the gym. For each team, the six cards bearing exercises and inspirational sayings should be scattered on the floor at half-court directly opposite the team (from the end line to the half-court line). Each set of six cards can have the same exercises and quotes; or, if you are really excited about this game, then all the cards can be different!

When the music begins, one team member runs out, picks one card from the team's group of cards, and brings it back to the team. The team members perform the indicated exercise for the indicated number of repetitions, then jog a lap together. No one may run ahead; the team must stay together. When the lap has been completed, another team member runs to the scattered cards and brings a card back to the team. The team again performs the indicated exercise, then runs a lap. This process continues until each team has picked up and implemented all of its cards.

Each team then circles up and reads each inspirational saying on its cards. Team members then pick their favorite quotation, as a team, and prepare to explain it to the class. After about five minutes of team discussion, each group reports to the class about its favorite quotation. It's fine if a quotation is used more than once; each team that uses it may have a different interpretation of it. An example of a card bearing an exercise and a quotation is included in the web resource, along with additional quotations. You can use them with your own favorite exercises and activities; of course, you can also use your own favorite quotations.

Inspirational Sayings for Inspirational Race Game

Sample Card Content
- Side 1: Teammates encourage one another while doing 15 push-ups. Try full push-ups before dropping to your knees.
- Side 2: *Anger must be the energy that has not yet found its right channels.*
  —Florida Scott Maxwell, *The Measure of My Days* (1968)

Inspirational Sayings
Here are some more inspirational quotations—just add an activity and a number to each card.

Everyone is endowed with qualities of a champion and can succeed in spite of handicaps in the most important game of all—the game of life.
—Alice Marble, tennis pioneer

When we judge or criticize another person, it says nothing about that person; it merely says something about our own need to be critical.
—Richard Carlson, *Don't Sweat the Small Stuff...and It's All Small Stuff* (1997)

Take chances, make mistakes. That's how you grow. Pain nourishes your courage. You have to fail in order to practice being brave.
—Mary Tyler Moore, legendary actress (quoted in *The Edge*, Howard Ferguson, 1990)

Reputation is what you're perceived to be. Character is what you really are.
—John Wooden, NBA basketball coach legend (quoted in *Playbook for Success*, Nancy Lieberman, 2010)

From L. Anderson and D.R. Glover, 2017, *Building character, community, and a growth mindset in physical education web resource.* (Champaign, IL: Human Kinetics).

Variations

- Use different sayings.
- Time the activity to see how fast teams can accomplish the task or set class records.
- Put out enough cards for each team member to go twice.
- Have the teams do another round but this time choose a different quotation.

Integrity Tag

Equipment

- Four to six colorful vests
- Three index cards that each have one positive character trait
- Three index cards that each have one negative character trait
- Method for affixing cards to vests (e.g., pins, clothespins, tape)
- Favorite gym music
- Tagging noodles (optional)

Description

After students have done a warm-up and gathered with their teams, tell them that you are going to say some words or phrases and that you would like them to say the opposite of each one. Now say some phrases indicative of positive character traits (e.g., "good sport") and ask the students to say the opposite (e.g., "poor sport"). Other examples include honesty (dishonesty), confidence (self-doubt), and integrity (cheating). Of course, your students may give various responses for the same meaning, and you can work with them to identify the best opposite meaning.

Now, select three of the negative (opposite) traits (e.g., poor sport, dishonesty, cheating), write one word on each set of three index cards, and attach the cards to vests (one card per vest). Select three students wearing the vests to serve as taggers; when they tag another student, that student must freeze. Do the same with the positive character traits. That is, write one trait (e.g., good sport, honesty, integrity) that corresponds with the three chosen negative traits on each set of index cards and attach the cards to vests of a different color. Again select three students wearing these vests to serve as "unfreezers"; when they give a frozen teammate a high five, they free the frozen student to rejoin the game.

To initiate the activity, have all of the students spread out in the gym. When the music begins, the three taggers try to tag as many students as they can. If your students are in the primary grades, you may want to tag with a noodle as it is a bit safer. If a student is tagged, he or she must freeze until freed by an unfreezer. Let the game continue for a while, then stop the music and let other children assume the roles of tagger and unfreezer.

Here are some discussion questions to use after the game.

- What happened when a tagger with a negative character trait tagged you? (Possible responses include the following: "We were frozen." "We couldn't move.")
- Have you ever seen or experienced a negative character trait affecting a team? What happens to a team when it has members with a negative character trait? (Students may answer to this effect: "They couldn't get along." "I saw a team arguing." "The team can't do well because they don't work well together—it's almost like being frozen.")
- How does a poor sport affect his or her own team? Give some examples.
- How might dishonesty affect a game?

This discussion can go on as long as you find it to be productive.

Variations

- Use different character-education words.
- Change the way in which students move.
- Have students say thank you when someone unfreezes them.

Character-Education Treasure Hunt

Adapted, by permission, from D.R. Glover and L.A. Anderson, 2003, *Character education: 43 fitness activities for community building* (Champaign, IL: Human Kinetics), 89-90.

Equipment

- Twenty-four index cards (four identical sets of six), each bearing a character-education focus word, an activity and number of reps, and a point value (as in the examples provided in the web resource)
- Four containers (boxes or buckets)
- Paper and pencil for each team
- Four cones to mark the path
- Twenty-four poly spots

Description

Hide all of the cards around the gym under the poly spots. Place the four containers in a circle in the middle of the gym. The objective of the game is to collect six different focus words.

Have students gather with their respective teams, each at its assigned container. One student from each team is designated by the team as the hunter. On your signal, each team starts jogging together around the perimeter of the gym. On a second signal from you, the hunters venture away from their teams in search of a character education card. When a hunter finds a card, he or she calls the team to that spot and everyone performs the activity indicated on the card. The hunter then puts the card in the team's container and rejoins the team in moving around the gym. Each hunter is allowed to find and turn over only one card; if it duplicates a card that the team has already put in its container, then the hunter rejoins the team empty-handed to wait for your next signal.

When all hunters have rejoined their teams, let the teams jog a bit more and then give another signal. On this signal, a new hunter ventures forth and looks for a new card, and so the process continues. The game ends when all of the team's six focus-word cards have been placed in the team's container and the team figures out the total point value of its cards. Wouldn't it be great to hear students yelling to a hunter, "We need *respect*! Find *respect*!" The web resource includes the cards you will need for this activity.

Character-Education Treasure Hunt

Make four sets of these cards.

Card 1	Card 2
10 points	6 points
10 push-ups	10 crunches
Respect	Honesty

Card 3	Card 4
5 points	3 points
20 jumping jacks	Touch all four walls in the gym; go as a team (no one may run ahead)
Patience	Resilience

Card 5	Card 6
2 points	1 point
1 lap of jogging as a team	10 burpees
Pride	Perseverance

From L. Anderson and D.R. Glover, 2017, *Building character, community, and a growth mindset in physical education web resource* (Champaign, IL: Human Kinetics).

Variations

- Hide the cards not only under poly spots but also under mats, pins, balls, bases, and so on. This approach makes the game more exciting by testing students' memories as they try to recall where their teammates have looked in order to avoid duplication.

- Use the numbers on the cards to integrate math into the activity; give each team a paper and pencil and require the teams to show their addition work at the end of the game. For older kids, have them perform multiplication and division using the numbers on the cards. Figure out ways to challenge them!

- Have teams track the number of laps that they jog or walk and try to improve on their past performances.

Work Together and Get Things Done

This is one of those activities where you make some of the needed equipment. You might get some help from a teaching assistant or inquire about whether it could be done as a project in an art class.

Equipment

- Individual laminated letters, at least 6 inches (15 cm) tall, sufficient to spell *pride* four times (i.e., four each of *p*, *r*, *i*, *d*, and *e*)
- Four plastic hoops (one for each team)
- Twenty-four index cards, each bearing an activity and the number of repetitions for the team as a whole (not each individual member) to complete (e.g., 100 sit-ups)
- Equipment needed for each activity (e.g., mats, basketballs, jump ropes)

Description

Each team tries to earn the letters needed to spell the word *pride*. Once a team has completed its team break, it can retrieve an activity card. You can place the cards around the gym or in the center circle; you can also have the teams get cards from you. Once a team has retrieved an activity card, it does the following:

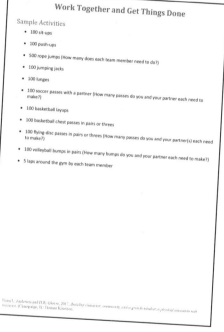

- Read the card carefully before attempting the activity (see the web resource).
- Complete each exercise or activity fully as a group.
- Ensure that each group member participates in each activity. However, it is not necessary for each team member to do the same amount of activity; it is up to the team to decide what each person does.
- Once the activity card task is completed, return the card to its original location (either in the gym or with you).
- Once a team has completed an activity and returned the card to its original place, it can retrieve a letter, which starts the process of spelling the word *pride*.

- Repeat the preceding steps to earn more letters; keep repeating until all activities have been completed and the word *pride* has been spelled.
- All activities must be done as a team, and each team member's efforts contribute to the number of reps indicated on the card. No team member should leave an activity until all team members are done.
- Some team members may do more than an equal share of a given activity if that strategy is agreed on by the team.
- When a team earns the last letter needed to spell *pride*, the team members exchange a round of high fives and then sit in a circle around their hoop with the word *pride* in the center.

Postactivity Discussion

When all teams are done, ask the following discussion questions about pride:

- What is pride?
- How can you take pride in your behavior?
- How can you take pride in how you act toward others?
- How do you cheat yourself if you do not do your best?
- How can an athlete take pride in preparing for his or her chosen sport?
- How can students take pride in their schoolwork?
- When you do your best, how do you feel?
- What does *pride* mean to you?
- Is pride earned or given? How so?
- Did your group or team take pride in your performance during this activity? How so?

Variation

The team must do one lap together before getting a new activity card.

Slovenian Relay

We call this the Slovenian relay because we introduced it at a workshop in Slovenia. It worked well there, and we think you will enjoy it too!

Equipment

- Plastic hoop for each team
- Ten-letter focus word for each team (not revealed to the team)
- Index cards (as in the example shown here), each bearing on the front side one letter of one of the focus words (i.e., ten index cards for each team) and a number corresponding to its team (e.g., team 1, team 2) and bearing on the back side a question addressing the relevant focus word (but not mentioning the word itself)

Description

Line up the teams behind the end line of the basketball court with each team gathered around its plastic hoop. If you want students to be more active, divide each team into two subgroups that each have only three or four members. In that case, of course, you will need to make more cards, but your students will get a great workout! Lay all of the focus cards facedown (i.e., with the letter and number down) along the half-court line. Mix the cards up to avoid having any group's cards all positioned together.

On your signal, the first person from each team runs to the cards and turns one over. If its number matches the team's number, the student takes it back to the team and places it in the team's hoop. The runner then high-fives the second runner, who runs to the card supply and turns over another card. If, on the other hand, the card number does not match, the runner leaves it in its original position and returns to the group empty-handed. This process continues until all letters of each word have been gathered by their corresponding team.

#1 G

What is your word?

What does the team think this word means?

Do you show this character trait? How?

Give me an example of someone who displays this character trait. Why did you choose him or her?

How do you feel when you are able to be what this word means?

Rules

1. Each team member can turn over only one card.

2. Only one team member can retrieve a card at a time.

3. The first team to figure out its word and spell it correctly wins the relay.

4. Once a team has spelled its word correctly, the team members hold a discussion by answering the questions on the backs of the cards. (You can create as many questions as you like and put the questions on the back of each card.)

Here are some suggested ten-letter focus words to use:

Some teachers dislike relays simply because they involve waiting for a turn. This relay, however, involves a lot of repetitions; in addition, when a student is waiting for a turn to retrieve a card, he or she is still involved in trying to figure

Discipline	Confidence
Enthusiasm	Initiative
Motivation	Resilience
Generosity	Respectful

out the team's word. As mentioned earlier, you can also increase the physical activity involved by dividing each team into two subgroups.

Variations

- Tell each team its word before the relay starts; each team must then bring back the letters in the proper order to spell the word.

- To increase the level of activity, write an exercise on each card in addition to what is already on the card and require the team to perform that exercise before retrieving another card. Alternatively, require the team to do one lap together before retrieving another card.

- After all teams have completed their words, rotate the teams so that each team has a new number and a new word, and then start again.

Reflection-Scenario Matching Game

This game combines focus words with reflection scenarios. It can be made into a race or, by using the variations, a quite vigorous game.

Equipment

- At least six index cards per team, each with a unique reflection scenario (either from the web resource or of your own creation) that addresses a character trait (e.g., honesty, respect, caring)
- At least 20 laminated focus-word posters (one word per poster), either from the web resource or of your own choice
- Poly spot for each team

Description

Place the focus-word posters on the floor next to one wall. Place the reflection-scenario cards facedown in the center of the gym, either scattered inside the center basketball circle or in a space that is 4 feet (1.2 m) square. Scatter the teams around the gym, each sitting in a circle around its poly spot and awaiting the signal to start the game.

On your signal, one member of each team runs to the center of the gym, retrieves a reflection-scenario card, runs back to the team's spot, and reads the scenario to the team. The team then comes to consensus as to what focus word the reflection scenario fits best. This task can prove difficult, because some reflection scenarios can fit several focus words. Once the team agrees on a word, the team members run together to the agreed-on word and place their reflection-scenario card on top of it. The team then runs back to its poly spot, whereupon another team member runs to the center to retrieve another reflection scenario card, and again the team works to agree on which focus word the card addresses.

This process continues until each team has placed six reflection-scenario cards on focus-word posters. Once all teams are done, start the activity again. This time, however, each team must pick new reflection-scenario cards. (If a team gets a card it has already used, the card must be put back in the circle.)

Reflection-Scenario Matching Game	
Sample Focus Words *Enlarge and laminate each word.*	
Responsibility	Sharing
Caring	Perseverance
Patience	Loyalty
Self-discipline	Dependability
Citizenship	Generosity
Honesty	Determination
Courage	Fairness
Sportsmanship	Respect
Integrity	Tolerance
Initiative	Forgiveness

From L. Anderson and D.R. Glover, 2017, *Building character, community, and a growth mindset in physical education web resource* (Champaign, IL: Human Kinetics).

Variations

- Before returning to their poly spot, each team's members must complete one lap (or 10 push-ups, 20 rope jumps, or 20 basketball passes—whatever task you like). Again, the teams must stay together; no one may run ahead.
- Put a question about the scenario on the back of each reflection-scenario card for team members to discuss before returning to their poly spot.

Character-Education Puzzle

Equipment

- Three plastic hoops: one for focus words, one for reflection scenarios, and one for inspirational sayings
- Character-education charts (one for each team), each divided into three columns: focus words, reflection scenarios, and inspirational sayings
- Twenty-four index cards—eight with a focus word, eight with a reflection scenario, and eight with an inspirational saying
- Chart listing 20 exercises or activities (available in the web resource) and either posted on the wall (large chart) or handed to each team (smaller printed chart)
- Two dice per team

Description

Place the focus words, reflection scenarios, and inspirational sayings in their respective hoops. Position the hoops about 20 feet (6 m) away from each other along one end line of the gym. Position the four teams at the other end of the gym with each sitting in a circle around its character-education chart and its activity chart (unless the activities are listed on a large chart posted on a wall). On your signal, each team rolls its dice to determine the number of repetitions to perform. The team members then pick an exercise from the activities chart and do the number of reps indicated by the dice.

When finished with the activity, the team jogs one lap around the outside of the gym together. Along the way, the team members stop briefly at the hoops at the other end of the gym to pick either one focus word, one reflection scenario, or one inspirational saying before continuing on their lap. Once back at their character-education chart, they place the index card in the correct position on the chart. Another team member then rolls the dice and picks the next activity. This process continues until the chart is completely filled, or each team has brought back six cards (two from each hoop). Each team's members then sit in a circle and decide on meanings for the focus words, inspirational sayings, and reflection scenarios on all of the index cards they have brought back.

Character-Education Puzzle

Exercise Activity Chart
1. Rope jump
2. Push-up
3. Sit-up
4. Jumping jack
5. Squat thrust or burpee
6. Squat jump
7. Side lunge
8. Forward lunge (alternating sides)
9. Inchworm
10. Starter exercise
11. Cone weave
12. Width-of-gym sprint
13. Layup
14. Gym scooter width of gym (prone)
15. Cone-to-cone bear walk
16. Arm circle (in both directions)
17. Windmill
18. Calf raise
19. Long jump
20. Tuck jump

From L. Andrews and D.R. Glover, 2013, *Building character, community, and a growth mindset in physical education web resource.* (Champaign, IL: Human Kinetics).

After about five minutes of team discussion, you might ask the following questions:

1. What do each of your focus words mean?
2. What character trait does your reflection scenario portray? Read your scenario and tell the class why you picked that trait.
3. Read one of your inspirational sayings to the class and tell us in your own words what you think it means.

The discussion may branch off when the teams report to the class. If so, that's great—talking about character puts the emphasis right where we want it!

Variations

- Keep track of every team's time so that each team can try to go faster the next time they do the activity.
- Add more spaces to the character-education chart so that each team retrieves three cards from each hoop.
- Repeat the activity and require students to draw different cards from each hoop (i.e., no repeats of the last round).

Character-Education Fitness Tag

Equipment

- Four foam balls (or beanbags, foam noodles, or other objects) to be used for tagging, each displaying a character-education focus word
- Place one definition poster on each wall and display the definition of each focus word (from the web resource or your choice), as well as activity directions (e.g., 20 jumping jacks and one lap of jogging; or 20 rope jumps and one lap of jogging)

Description

Choose four people to serve as taggers and provide each one with a focus-word tagging implement. On your signal (e.g., music or just saying "go"), the taggers tag as many people as possible with their focus-word implements. When tagged, a student must figure out which poster definition matches the tagging implement, then do the activity indicated on the poster. Upon completing the activity, the student rejoins the game. After a certain period of time passes, select four new taggers and continue the game.

When you decide that the game has gone on long enough, stop it and instruct students to partner up with one or two of their teammates for a "walk-and-talk." This portion involves walking two laps around the gym while discussing the

Character-Education Fitness Tag

Focus Words

The following focus words are for the taggers. You need only four taggers at a time; tape a word to each tagger.

Tolerance	Trust
Pride	Discipline
Loyalty	Caring
Respect	Patience
Honesty	Citizenship

four focus words and definitions. To facilitate their talk, provide them with discussion questions. Here are some very general samples; if you prefer, make them more specific to your chosen focus words.

- Have you ever displayed _____ (focus word) during class? If so, how did you do it?
- Do you think _____ (focus word) is an important quality to have? Why?
- What is the opposite of _____ (focus word)? What do you think when you see that behavior? Have you ever displayed it? How did you feel about that?

Variation

Have eight focus words ready and switch to four new focus words for the next round but still use only four at a time.

Teamwork

Equipment

- Four plastic hoops
- Four charts (one for each team), each with six focus words (examples available in the web resource)
- Twenty-four index cards, each indicating an activity and giving a focus-word definition (examples available in the web resource)
- Four additional plastic hoops, each of which will hold six focus-word definition cards
- Sixteen jump ropes
- Sixteen sets of sport equipment (e.g., basketballs, floor hockey sticks and pucks, soccer balls), depending on your current unit
- Four mats (two for sit-ups, two for push-ups)

Description

Position the teams along one end of the gym, spread out enough that they do not intrude on each other's space. Each team has a focus-word chart, which is placed at the center of the team's plastic hoop; each chart lists all six of the team's focus words. Each team is assigned a team number (1 through 4). Each team also has a set of cards bearing focus-word definitions and activities in a hoop placed in the middle of the gym, directly across from the team. Each team's definitions match the team's focus words.

On your signal, each team jogs to its hoop containing focus-word definitions and works to decide which definition matches the first word on the team's focus-word chart. Once the team members have identified the correct definition, they take the card back to their starting hoop and put it facedown on the floor beside the focus-word chart. The team members then perform the exercise indicated on the definition card. When the exercise is complete, they jog back to the definitions hoop and come to a consensus regarding the definition of the second focus word on their chart. This process continues until all six focus words have been matched with their respective definitions and all of the indicated activities have been completed. When every team has finished, instruct the teams to rotate hoops and do another round.

Teamwork

Focus-Word Charts

Cut apart the charts, and place one chart in each team's hoop.

Team 1	Team 2	Team 3	Team 4
Courtesy	Citizenship	Kindness	Resourceful
Punctuality	Sportsmanship	Cleanliness	Honesty
Responsibility	Gratitude	Resilience	Respect
Civility	Patriotism	Flexibility	Tolerance
Reliability	Compassion	Diligence	Loyalty
Honor	Generosity	Initiative	Courage

From L. Anderson and D.R. Glover, 2017, *Building character, community, and a growth mindset in physical education with web resource* (Champaign, IL: Human Kinetics).

Character Construction

Equipment

- Forty-eight (twelve for each team) buckets (e.g., 5-gallon [19-liter] buckets obtained from the school cafeteria or custodial supply). Using a permanent marker, write one focus word on the outside of each bucket; also number the buckets from 1 through 12. If you cannot find enough buckets, you could use stacking cups with a focus word and number taped or written on each cup.
- Building blueprints for each team (as in the sample illustration) showing different patterns in which the buckets can be stacked

Description

This game is great fun and combines practice in team communication skills with team planning. The objective is to build various pyramids with the buckets. Designate a starting area for each team and stack the buckets there in two columns of six each. About 50 feet (15 m) away, designate a finish area where students will build their pyramids. Designate another location (e.g., hoop, mat) to serve as the construction office.

Let each team determine which members will serve as builders and which will serve as construction managers (no more than eight members per team). For a team of eight students, six serve as builders and two as construction man-

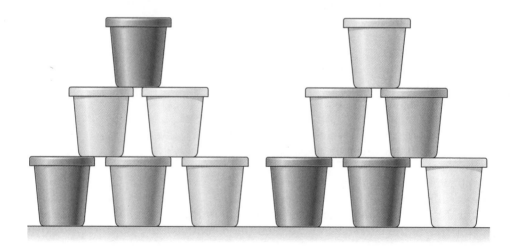

agers; a team of six designates only one construction manager. Give the construction blueprints to the managers, who must stay in the construction office; they may not touch the builders or the buckets. When the builders are ready, the managers give stacking instructions to them according to the blueprint.

Builders may move only one bucket at a time to the construction site. When instructing the builders, managers must call each builder by his or her first name and use the focus word printed on the bucket. Construction managers may not use the terms *line*, *top*, *front*, and *behind*.

Variations

- The construction manager must use only the character-education focus words to describe buckets.
- When the manager calls out a word, the team must give the word's definition before picking up the corresponding bucket.
- The construction manager must use only the bucket numbers to designate buckets.
- Set a time limit for construction.
- The construction manager must use math equations to designate buckets. Here is an example: "Use bucket 2 plus 2 plus 5 minus 1" (i.e., bucket 8).
- Increase the distance between the starting area and the construction area.
- Construction managers must call out a different way to move from the starting area to the construction area each time a builder moves a bucket.
- After each bucket is placed, the team must perform an exercise, run a lap, or make a basket.

Beanbag Toss for Character

Equipment

- Twenty-four plastic hoops and floor tape for securing them
- As many beanbags as you can find (at least one per student)
- Twenty-four index cards (one for each hoop), each bearing one focus word (examples available in the web resource)
- Eight poly spots

Description

For the purpose of this game, divide each regular team into two smaller teams. This description is written for eight teams and three hoops per team. Each smaller team lines up behind one end line of the gym. (The game can also be played using the width of the gym, which may give each team more room if you have a small gym.) Each team has a poly spot to mark its starting point, and each student has at least one beanbag. The immediate object of the game is to toss beanbags underhand into the hoops, which are arranged in single file in front of each team and secured to the floor with floor tape.

More specifically, each team's hoops are arranged in a straight line, with each successive hoop located farther from the tossers. Each team tries to get all three focus words back to its poly spot before the other teams do. To obtain a focus word, a team must land at least three beanbags in a given hoop in one round. The team can then collect the focus word in that hoop and turn its efforts toward the next hoop. Tossers can toss one at a time or all together, whichever you decide. If a team does not get three beanbags in a given hoop, it must collect its beanbags and try again for that hoop.

Once a team has collected all three focus words, the team members sit in a small circle and create a reflection scenario that addresses the focus word that they choose from the three cards collected. When all teams are finished, put the focus words back into the hoops, have the teams rotate, and start a new game.

Focus Words for Beanbag Toss for Character		
Respect	Poise	Commitment
Honesty	Class	Discipline
Sportsmanship	Loyalty	Principles
Trustworthiness	Unselfishness	Tolerance
Judgment	Caring	Patience
Pride	Enthusiasm	Compassion
Integrity	Courage	Citizenship
Character	Confidence	Learned

From L. Anderson and B.R. Glover, 2017, *Building character, community, and a winning mindset in physical education with resources* (Champaign, IL: Human Kinetics).

Variations

- Make the toss more challenging by placing the last hoop at about half-court.
- Put numbers on the focus words to integrate suitable math problems.
- Instead of focus words, use reflection scenarios or inspirational sayings.
- After a team collects its beanbags, the team members must run to the far wall and then back to their poly spot before proceeding to the next set of tosses.
- Everyone tosses on your signal, or one person per team tosses on your signal.
- Play across the width of the gym instead of the length.
- Give each hoop a value (e.g., 3, 5, 10) and see which team gets to 100 first.

Rubber Ducks

Equipment

- Forty small rubber ducks (or tennis balls or other objects), each with a character-education focus word taped to it (examples available in the web resource)
- Four basketballs for each team
- Four baskets
- Sixteen poly spots
- Four plastic hoops
- One sheet of definitions of character-education terms (available in the web resource)
- Forty index cards, each marked with a character-education focus word and definition (see the web resource)
- Four pencils
- Your favorite gym music

Description

Each team sits in a circle around a plastic hoop at the top of the basketball key (i.e., the free throw area). In the center of each team's hoop are its character-education definition worksheet and a pencil. Each basket area has four poly spots arranged in a semicircle around the basket. (The distance from the basket should be determined by the students' age.) Each team has four basketballs, and team members take turns shooting from the poly spots; they keep an accurate record of the number of shots made.

When you start the music, the teams begin shooting baskets. Each team must make a total of 10 baskets from the poly spots under its basket. The team then puts its balls down and rushes to the center of the gym to collect 10 character education ducks from the center circle. Each team member must bring back at least one duck; some teammates may have to bring back two. When the team gets the ducks back to its hoop, the team members match the focus word on each duck to the correct definition on the worksheet, then write the word on the sheet beside the correct definition.

Rubber Ducks

Worksheet

1. _____ — Consistent attention to high-quality work; ability to remain focused on a goal
2. _____ — Proactiveness; ability to think and take action on one's own
3. _____ — Cleverness, creativity, imagination, or inventiveness
4. _____ — Respect for individual differences, views, beliefs, and skills
5. _____ — Recognition of diversity and the opinions, practices, and beliefs of others
6. _____ — Working together for a common purpose
7. _____ — Ability or act of letting go of resentment
8. _____ — Equal treatment of and behavior toward others and their viewpoints
9. _____ — Obligation or pledge to carry out an action or to support a policy or person
10. _____ — Pleasantness, good spirits, good feeling
11. _____ — Desire to move or work toward a goal
12. _____ — Inner strength to pursue a goal or task; willpower
13. _____ — Ability to work hard without giving up
14. _____ — Adherence to a code of moral or ethical behavior; consistent truthfulness and fairness

From L. Anderson and D.R. Glover, 2017, *Building character, community, and a growth mindset in physical education web resource.* (Champaign, IL: Human Kinetics).

The team then checks its work by having each team member take one rubber duck and spreading out to find the matching index card. The cards, each marked with a focus word and its definition, are scattered facedown around the outside of the gym, near the walls. When a team member finds a matching card, he or she takes it back to check the answer on the worksheet. If the card matches the worksheet definition, the card is placed inside the hoop; if not, it is taken back to its original position and the team member continues searching. The game ends when all teams have gathered all 10 matching cards inside their respective hoops and all written answers on the worksheet are correct.

Variations

- Time the activity or have teams race to see which team can complete its worksheet correctly first.
- Put numbers on the ducks, have each team add up its numbers, and write the total on its worksheet.
- After finding a matching card, the student must do one lap before taking the card to the team hoop.
- Indicate an exercise on each card; when a card is used, the exercise must be performed.

Character-Education Basketball

Equipment

- Eight containers (e.g., pails, buckets, boxes, or combination thereof)
- Forty-eight index cards, each bearing a character-education focus word (examples available in the web resource)
- Eight basketballs
- Six basketball hoops
- Your favorite gym music

Description

Divide each regular team into smaller teams (e.g., eight teams of three); or if you have five teams of six in your class, divide them into ten teams of three. Each team gathers around a container, and the teams are equidistant from the gym's center circle, where the focus-word cards are scattered facedown.

Start the music to begin the game, whereupon one member of each team dribbles to the center circle, picks up one focus-word card, dribbles back to the team, and puts the card in the team's container. All three team members then run to their designated basket, where each team member must try to make five layups. Students should encourage teammates who are having trouble, and they may not return to their box and retrieve another focus word until each member makes five layups (or until an agreed upon amount of time has elapsed).

Once the team returns to its box, another team member dribbles to the center to retrieve another focus word. This process continues until all focus-word cards are gone. Each team now works to figure out the definition of each focus word it has collected. Allow about five minutes for this work, then have each team report its results to the rest of the class.

Focus Words for Character-Education Basketball		
Caring	Respect	Compassion
Perseverance	Courage	Resourcefulness
Patience	Tolerance	Courtesy
Loyalty	Integrity	Self-confidence
Discipline	Character	Gratitude
Trust	Pride	Flexibility
Citizenship	Confidence	Diligence
Generosity	Initiative	Trustworthiness
Honesty	Forgiveness	Civility
Determination	Resilience	Punctuality
Sportsmanship	Kindness	Honor

From E. Andersen and D.R. Glover, 2017, *Building character, community, and a growth mindset in physical education*, web resource (Champaign, IL: Human Kinetics).

Variations

- Use inspirational sayings rather than focus words on the index cards (see the web resource for chapter 3).
- Declare as the winner the team with the most focus words collected.
- Use equipment other than basketballs; for example, require each team to make 20 football passes.

SUMMARY

The main purpose of physical education is to help students develop literacy in fitness and skill development. At the same time, because physical education is a favorite subject for many students, physical education teachers are a natural fit for leadership roles in facilitating schoolwide initiatives. Putting these two realities together, imagine a school that sets a collective goal of equipping students with the tools needed to live healthy lives and grow into people of integrity. These two goals are both achievable and can be facilitated by implementing ideas presented in this chapter.

On the other hand, as mentioned in previous chapters, physical educators and coaches typically have not had experience or background in techniques for teaching social skills. Instead, the main emphasis has been placed on movement and skill acquisition. We need to recognize that when social skills are stressed and taught with the same vigor as physical skills, we can help students experience more success in both areas simply because of the motivational effect. Indeed, when we create environments that students are excited to be a part of, they invest more readily in accomplishing both collective and individual goals. By using engaging activities to teach students what strong character looks like, sounds like, and feels like, we enable them to increase their knowledge and create stronger bonds between classmates and teammates.

Team-Building Challenges

The way a team plays as a whole determines its success.
You may have the greatest bunch of individual stars
in the world, but if they don't play together,
the club won't be worth a dime.

Babe Ruth, MLB baseball legend

Team building is one of the best ways to facilitate the skills necessary to achieve goals and win championships. Research supports the deceptively simple wisdom expressed in Babe Ruth's statement that a group is much more effective when it is characterized by trust and strong bonds. Too often, however, teachers and coaches assume that teamwork automatically happens when a group of kids are put together to form a team. To the contrary, we have learned—through years and years of experience—that the most successful teams have coaches who emphasize, teach, and practice the skills necessary to create a cohesive team. With that knowledge in mind, this chapter provides physical challenges that strengthen the bonds among team members; just as important, they prompt teams to address the challenges that often contribute to breakdown and dysfunction.

The team challenges presented here also allow students to collaboratively practice a growth mindset, which is essential to maximizing growth in both individuals and teams. More specifically, students need to approach obstacles as opportunities for improvement and to approach failure as a necessary component of ultimate success. However, these concepts of a growth mindset do not come naturally for anyone, especially children. As a result, they must be deliberately taught, practiced, and reinforced.

One of the benefits of team-building activities derives from the fact that, inevitably, teams face obstacles and experience failure. These instances of adversity give students opportunities to learn how to handle frustration, avoid breakdown and blame, pull together to achieve their common goal. For these reasons, you must include team building in your program if you want to maximize the performance of your individuals and teams.

One of the many skills that students gain from team-building activities is that of collaboratively solving problems in the face of adversity. What a powerful trait you equip your students with by helping them develop the skills necessary to succeed in the challenges presented here! As an educator or coach, you hold the power to teach students the skills necessary to build one another up and recognize how individual efforts can make a team stronger. In order to realize these benefits, students must learn to manage frustration and impulsive reactions, think creatively to solve problems, handle failure, work together, take risks, and learn how to lead effectively.

Most of the team-building challenges presented in this chapter are designed to be done outdoors. If you would like to explore team building further, check out *Essentials of Team Building* by Daniel W. Midura and Donald R. Glover (Human Kinetics, 2005).

TEAM ROLES

Our understanding of how best to facilitate the team-building unit has changed over the past 30 years. When we first began, we simply put students in teams, presented them with a challenge, and watched them try to solve it. We did not teach them how to function as respectful, tolerant teammates; we thought that would happen as a by-product of the experience. We did tell students that the *process* of solving a challenge was as important as completing it. We also constantly stressed cooperation, and we conducted a short discussion after the challenges to help students gain perspective as to how their teams functioned during the challenge. But that was all. My, how we have evolved!

We now believe that team building should be the first unit that a teacher implements at the start of the school year, even if only for two days. The precursors to team building are the discussions and activities addressed in chapter 2. Students must learn how to support their teammates through praise and encouragement before embarking on problem-solving challenges. They also need to be introduced to the attitudes of a growth mindset that are necessary for overcoming adversity (as explored in greater detail in chapter 6). Even though team building can be taught as a unit in itself, the team-building challenges should be revisited periodically throughout the year (monthly or quarterly) to help students refresh their teamwork skills and growth mindset.

For team challenges, assign each of the following key roles to one member of each team:

- Organizer
- Encourager
- Praiser
- Recorder

The following sections address each of these roles, along with your role as the teacher.

Organizer

The team-organizer role is a leadership opportunity—a chance to serve as captain for a given challenge. Once a team has decided which challenge to attempt, the organizer picks up the challenge card. (All challenge cards for the challenges presented here are provided in the chapter's web resource.) The organizer either reads the challenge to the team or has someone else read it. If the team has any questions, the organizer (the team captain) can approach you for clarification. To help students understand the challenge, you may wish to include some clarification questions on the challenge card for the organizer to ask the team; the organizer decides if the team answers the questions thoroughly enough to begin the challenge.

Reading the challenge card (or choosing someone else to read it) gives the organizer a leadership experience right away. It may not be easy to read and explain the challenge to the group, but hopefully, everyone on the team will take his or her turn. If the organizer does not feel comfortable reading in front of the group, he or she may give the challenge card to a teammate to read. When the challenge is over and the team rotates to a new challenge, the organizer from the just-completed challenge appoints a new organizer; thus a new leadership opportunity begins.

Encourager

By now, your students should have a pretty good idea of what encouragement involves and how powerful it can be. The role of encourager, like that of organizer, should rotate among team members as the team goes through challenges. We hope that all team members will encourage each other, but the person assigned to that role *must* encourage at least one person before the completion of the challenge. We assign this function as a role when students first start team building; as the unit progresses, this role may disappear as encouragement becomes a habit for all students.

Praiser

Your students should now know the difference between encouragement and praise; to review, encouragement is given during an attempt or in challenging situations. Specific praise is given after completion of an attempt or when recognizing the positive actions of others. The praiser should praise at least one person, either during the challenge or after it (e.g., "Way to go team—we really pulled together after failing the first few times!"). As with giving encouragement, giving praise offers students an opportunity to exercise leadership. It is not always easy to give compliments, or to hear praise directed to oneself, and some students are not used to it. Sadly, many students are more used to put-downs and sarcasm.

Recorder

The web resource for this chapter includes a sample team report card, which can serve as a simple assessment device. The report card includes four reflective questions to be asked by the recorder:

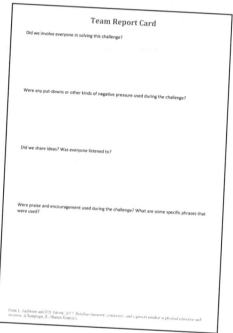

- How did we involve everyone in solving this challenge?
- Were any put-downs or other kinds of negative pressure used during the challenge?
- How were ideas shared? Was everyone listened to?
- How were praise and encouragement used during the challenge? What are some specific phrases that were used?

The team report card can be handled orally; alternatively, you might ask each recorder to write down some of the group's thoughts and turn them in. The team report card can be used either after each challenge or after several challenges, whichever you prefer. In order to participate more effectively in more challenges, we suggest doing a team report card after every third challenge. This will give the team a clearer picture of how they are doing as a team—it will show them some of the specific encouragement used and some things that could hold the team back. If a team has trouble working together, that is also a good time to use the report card or to revisit the team pacts introduced in chapter 2.

Teacher

The teacher's role in team-building activities has changed slightly over the years. True, you must remain firm in requiring that each group solve the challenge by following all of the rules. In addition, do not be too quick to help or give hints about how to solve the challenge. Students take great pride in their team if they have to struggle before eventually succeeding. Indeed, the learning often lies in the struggle. At the same time, teachers also need to reflect on team building more than has been typical in the past. When done right, reflection helps students form stronger teams and engage in more meaningful experiences.

To that end, ask questions such as the following: What gave your team the most difficulty during this challenge? What did you do to overcome that problem? How did encouragement affect your team's performance? What are some examples of encouragement that the team used? What traits of a growth mindset did the team demonstrate? Questions like these invite team members to reflect, and reflection is the glue that connects and seals students' learning.

Power of Six

Adapted, by permission, from Victoria A. Otto.

Equipment

Various shapes found on your school grounds (e.g., tree, rock, bush, branch, statue, wall, playground equipment)

Description

Each team performs a balance in which all team members are connected to each other and a total of only six body parts touch the ground. The balance also incorporates a piece of the landscape (e.g., tree, rock, playground equipment).

Rules

1. The team must try to build a balance in which all team members are connected.

2. Only six total body parts may touch the ground.

3. The team balance must incorporate a piece of the landscape that is approved by you.

4. If the team falls out of the balance, it must start over.

5. Each team must hold the balance until you give the okay to disassemble.

6. No one is allowed to use a teammate's last name or to use a put-down.

7. At the end of a successful balance, each student must high-five all team members.

Power of Six

Equipment

Various shapes found on your school grounds (e.g., tree, rock, bush, branch, statue, wall, playground equipment)

Starting Position

Group members work together to find the designated piece of equipment or landscape feature. Once they find it, they collaborate to make a connected six-point balance that incorporates the equipment landscape feature.

The Challenge

The group has completed the challenge when all members of the team—along with selected equipment or landscape feature—form a connected, stable, six-point balance. The group members should be able to hold the balance until the teacher releases them.

Rules

1. The team must try to build a balance in which all team members are connected.

2. Only six total body parts may touch the ground.

3. The team must incorporate some piece of the landscape or equipment that is approved by the teacher to be part of the balance.

4. If the team falls, it must start over. Each team must hold the balance or pose until the teacher gives the okay for them to disassemble.

5. No one is allowed to use a teammate's last name or to use a put-down.

6. Each student must high-five all teammates at the end of a successful balance.

Completion of the Task

A team has succeeded when the required number of body parts are touching the ground, and the group is connected in a stable balance that incorporates its chosen object.

From L. Anderson and D.R. Glover, 2017, *Building character, community, and a growth mindset in physical education web resource* (Champaign, IL: Human Kinetics).

Variations

- Challenge each team to complete three different balances before the end of the class.
- Require each team to change the number of body parts touching the ground each time it tries a new balance.
- Challenge each team to *flow* from one balance to another.
- Establish limits on how the balance must be performed; for example, of the six body parts touching the ground, no more than three can be feet.
- Assign one team member to serve as the photographer; this team member should snap a picture of the team balance to be posted in the gym.
- Change the number of body parts touching the ground according to the age of the students. For example, first graders may touch with twelve body parts, whereas eighth graders may touch only with five.

Lean on Me

Equipment

- One rope (regular rope or several clotheslines tied together) measuring at least 100 feet (30 m) for younger students and at least 130 feet (40 m) for high schoolers
- Enough vinyl bases or poly spots to mark a clearly defined standing space for each group member
- For each student, a card bearing either a character-education focus word or a definition matching one of the words (words and definitions available in the web resource for chapter 3)
- Large open area (perhaps outdoors) in which to conduct the challenge

Description

Lean on Me offers a distinctive challenge in that it can be attempted by a very large group. The group holds onto a rope in the shape of a circle; the ends of the rope should be tied together with a reliable square knot. The group members let go of the rope one pair at a time with the goal of getting down to the smallest number of people possible while still keeping the rope off the ground. Those supporting the rope must not move their feet, take their hands off of the rope, or slide their hands along the rope.

To get set up for the activity, group members space themselves evenly around the rope, then slide backward until the rope is taut. Now each student puts his or her poly spot on the floor and stands on it. Each group member holds onto the rope with two hands and with his or her elbows straight. In addition, each member has memorized a card with either a character-education word or a matching definition for one of the words.

To engage in the activity, group members decide which two students will let go of the rope at any given time. In order to let go, the students must match a focus word and its definition. In other words, a student who has memorized a character-education word may not let go until the group discusses (collaborates) and correctly identifies that word's correct definition. Once a match has been made, the student with the word and the student with its definition may both let go. The group continues to release matching pairs until they have successfully solved the challenge—that is, until only four group members are left holding the rope off the ground.

Rules

1. A group member may not step off of a base until he or she has released the rope. If you do this challenge outside, you will not use poly spots (they are not designed for asphalt or grass); however, students are still not allowed to shuffle their feet or take a step.

2. Once the task has started, group members may not remove their hands from the rope unless they have been selected to let go.

3. Group members may not slide their hands while holding the rope.

4. A pair of team members must match a character-education word with its definition before stepping off of the base. In addition, the entire team must be notified that the two students have matched and are going to let go. Only one pair of matching students may step off at a time.

5. Once a pair of team members has let go of the rope, those two students may not touch the rope again. They may assist or touch their teammates who are still holding the rope, but they may not touch the rope itself.

6. No one may call another team member by his or her last name or use a put-down.

7. If a rule is broken, or if the rope hits the floor, the challenge attempt must stop and the group must start over.

Variations

- Do not require that students match a word and definition before letting go. Instead, allow team members to let go of the rope one at a time and see if the group can get down to three members left holding the rope off the ground.

- Time the activity. How quickly can the group get down to three members left holding the rope?

Lean On Me

Equipment

- One rope (regular rope or several clotheslines tied together) measuring at least 100 feet (30 m) long for younger students and at least 130 feet long for high school students and securely tied using a good square knot

- Enough vinyl bases or poly spots to mark a clearly defined standing space for each group member

- For each student, a card bearing either a character-education focus word (e.g., respect, honesty) or a definition matching one of the words

Starting Position

All group members are spaced evenly around the rope, which is shaped in a circle with the ends securely tied to close the circle. Students hold onto the rope with two hands and slowly back up until the rope is taut. Each student places a poly spot under his or her feet. The group members then lean back. After the group begins the challenge, participants may not move their feet or hands unless they are chosen to let go. Each group member must remember his or her focus word or definition.

The Challenge

The group must decide which two members should let go of the rope at a given time. To do so, the group must choose two people with a matching focus-word card and definition card. This process continues until four people are left holding the rope off the ground.

Rules

1. A student may not step off of his or her base until it is his or her turn to release the rope.

2. Once the activity begins, students may not remove their hands from the rope unless they have been selected to let go.

3. Group members may not slide their hands onto the rope.

4. Before stepping off of a base, a pair of students must match a character-education focus word with its definition and notify the entire team that they have matched and are letting go. Only one matched pair can step off at a time.

5. Once a pair of team members lets go of the rope, they may not touch the rope again. They may assist and touch teammates still holding the rope, but they may not touch the rope itself.

5. No one may call another student by his or her last name or use a put-down.

From L. Anderson and D.R. Glover, 2017, *Building character, community, and a growth mindset in physical education with* resource. (Champaign, IL: Human Kinetics).

Team Stone Toss

Equipment

- One small, flat stone (i.e., skipping stone) per team member
- Twelve-inch (30-cm) poly spot for each team
- Starting line for each team marked by sidewalk chalk, if you are doing the activity on the playground; a rope will be a good starting line if you are on grass

Description

Select suitable stones yourself or have students do so by visiting an appropriate natural area. Sending students into a field to select their own stones can add a lot of interest to this challenge, but if your school grounds do not include access to a suitable area, you can visit a landscape center and pick out stones yourself. (Another alternative is to pick up washers at a hardware store, but stones are more fun!) Each student can then select his or her own stone from the collection you provide.

Once stones are selected, students gather with their teams behind their respective starting (tossing) lines. Each team's poly spot should be positioned 10 feet (3 m) from its tossing line, directly in front of the team. On your signal, the members of each team try to toss their stones so that they land on the team's poly spot. In order to complete the challenge, each team must get a designated number of stones to land on the spot (e.g., five of eight stones tossed). You can decide this number yourself or let the class decide.

Rules

1. Tosses must be done underhand.
2. A team member can toss only his or her own stone.
3. No one can use a teammate's last name or use a put-down.
4. Every team member should encourage or praise another team member at least once during the challenge.
5. When the challenge has been completed, teammates exchange high fives all around.

Variations

- Give all teams a designated number of attempts to get as many stones as possible on their respective poly spots (e.g., make five attempts, then count how many stones are on the spot).

- Use a 9-inch (23-cm) poly spot.

- Increase the tossing distance.

- For each team, position five poly spots 3 feet (1 m) apart in a row. The team tosses at each poly spot, trying to get at least one stone on one of the five poly spots. They continue tossing until they have at least one stone on each poly spot. Or, the teacher may decide to have students toss until all stones are on a spot. This means there may be more than one stone on a spot and some spots may not have a stone. Allow the teams to create their own challenge with the spots and stones. If a student gets his or her stone on the poly spot first, that student may not throw again; instead, he or she now plays the role of encourager.

- For younger students, use a carpet square; this will make the target bigger and the stone will stay in place after being tossed.

- Assign a point value to each poly spot. The first team to get to 50 points wins. This adds a bit of math to the challenge.

Team Stone Toss

Equipment

- One small, flat stone (i.e., skipping stone) per team member
- Twelve-inch (30-cm) poly spot for each team
- Starting line for each team (if you play on the playground, use sidewalk chalk to mark the line or an existing line on the playground. If you play in the grass, use a rope as the starting line.)

Starting Position

Each team gathers behind its starting line, and each team member has a selected stone ready to toss.

The Challenge

Each team tries to land a designated number of stones on its poly spot, which is positioned 10 feet (3 m) from the starting line.

Rules

1. Tosses must be done underhand.
2. A team member can toss only his or her own stone.
3. No one can use a teammate's last name or use a put-down.
4. Every team member should encourage or praise another team member at least once during the challenge.
5. When the challenge has been completed, teammates exchange high fives all around.

Completion of the Task

The task is completed when the team lands the required number of stones on the poly spot.

From L. Anderson and D.R. Glover. 2017. *Building character, community, and a growth mindset in physical education with resources.* (Champaign, IL: Human Kinetics).

I See Me

Adapted, by permission, from Paul Shirilla.

Equipment

Camera (preferably on a personal smartphone) for each student or pair of students; most students have a smartphone, so this would be an easy way to get more cameras into this challenge.

Description

This activity allows students to explore their own connection to nature, be creative, and engage in self-reflection.

Give students 15 to 20 minutes to simply wander outside and find something of visual interest. This activity does not have to be done in a special location. Encourage students to pay attention to small details in nature that they may often fail to notice. Once they have identified something of interest, they take a photo. Encourage highly focused images, rather than landscape shots or pictures of entire objects; this will encourage the students to notice details they often miss when looking at the big picture. Students then send their images to you electronically (via e-mail or text message).

After students have taken their pictures, ask them to respond to questions such as the following:

- Why did you choose this image? What about it caught your attention?
- How do you feel about this object?
- How is this object like you?
- How is this object not like you?

Once you obtain all of the images, organize them for a slideshow and share it with students during the next class meeting. First, show all of the images (set to music, if you like) without stopping or slowing down. Then show them again, this time stopping at each image and allowing students to each identify their own image and briefly discuss why they chose it.

Rules

1. This is an individual activity. Students should not work together unless they need to share a camera; if students do share a camera, they are still responsible for each taking their own individual image.
2. Inform students ahead of time that they will each share their image with the class and should be prepared to discuss why they chose it.
3. The images must show objects of natural (i.e., not human) origin.

Variations

- Instead of sending their images to you for sharing with the class, students can post them (and corresponding question responses if you like) to their social media accounts. This approach allows a higher degree of exposure and gives students a sense of ownership in the activity.
- Let the members of each team print their photos and then collaborate to make a large collage using tagboard and tape. Post their work in a school hallway.

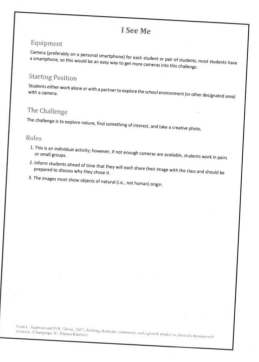

I See Me

Equipment

Camera (preferably on a personal smartphone) for each student or pair of students; most students have a smartphone, so this would be an easy way to get more cameras into this challenge.

Starting Position

Students either work alone or with a partner to explore the school environment (or other designated area) with a camera.

The Challenge

The challenge is to explore nature, find something of interest, and take a creative photo.

Rules

1. This is an individual activity; however, if not enough cameras are available, students work in pairs or small groups.
2. Inform students ahead of time that they will each share their image with the class and should be prepared to discuss why they chose it.
3. The images must show objects of natural (i.e., not human) origin.

From L. Anderson and D.R. Glover, 2017, *Building character, community, and a growth mindset in physical education with remotive.* (Champaign, IL: Human Kinetics).

Geocaching

Adapted, by permission, from Paul Shirilla.

Equipment

- One GPS unit (or smartphone geocaching app) per group
- Index cards bearing character-education inspirational sayings to place in containers

Description

Building on orienteering skills, geocaching provides an opportunity for students to use current technology while navigating outdoors. Although we often encourage students to spend time outside as a way to get away from screens and technology, this activity provides a good example of how nature and technology are sometimes compatible. In addition, students are often more comfortable with and interested in using a GPS unit or smartphone app rather than an old-fashioned compass. Thus this activity can also be used as a hook to get students interested in spending time outdoors.

In geocaching, individuals place containers or "caches" in outdoor locations and upload their GPS coordinates, along with clues, to a website. Such caches have been hidden all over the world, in both urban and rural environments. Of the several geocaching websites, the largest and most common is located at www.geocaching.com. The site's Learn tab offers several useful videos explaining the basics of geocaching and how to get started. We recommend allowing at least 30 minutes in class to show these videos to your students before heading outside to go geocaching.

Identify an outdoor location close to your school for this activity. Popular locations for caches include city, state, and regional parks, and it is common at such locations for several geocaches to be placed within a 1-mile (1.6-km) radius. This abundance allows students to hunt for more than one cache in a relatively short time. If you prefer to stay close to the school, you can construct your own geocaching course and upload the coordinates and clues to the geocaching.com site. Place the index cards with inspirational sayings at each cache site.

At the chosen location, divide each team into two groups. Allow the groups to find as many caches as they can in the time available.

Rules

1. Be sure that students replace geocaches exactly where they found them.

2. Students must stay together in their respective groups at all times and work together to find caches.

3. Take extra safety precautions since students will be out of your sight while searching for geocaches. Each group should have a working cell phone with which to contact you in case of emergency.

4. In case of an injury, one student should stay with the injured student while the others leave to find you and lead you to the injured student.

Variation

If time allows, students can place their own caches and upload the information to the geocaching.com website. Students can then work to find each other's caches.

Geocaching

Equipment
- One GPS unit (or smartphone geocaching app) per group
- Index cards bearing character-education inspirational saying to place in caches

Starting Position

Students are organized into small teams (three or four members each). Each team has a GPS unit or geocaching app. The teams are positioned at a starting point in a park or on school grounds.

The Challenge

Each team uses its GPS unit or geocaching app to follow the GPS course and collect or write down the inspirational sayings found at the caches.

Rules

1. Leave geocaches exactly where you found them.
2. Stay together in your respective groups at all times; work together to find the caches.
3. Take extra safety precautions since you will be out of the teacher's sight while searching for caches. Each group should have a working cell phone with which to contact the teacher in case of emergency.
4. In case of an injury, one student should stay with the injured student while the others leave to find the teacher and bring him or her to the injured student.

From L. Anderson and D.R. Glover, 2017, *Building character, community, and a growth mindset in physical education with sequences* (Champaign, IL: Human Kinetics).

Letterboxing

Adapted, by permission, from Paul Shirilla.

Equipment

- Written clues
- Character-education inspirational sayings

It is also possible to run this activity without equipment.

Description

Letterboxing is a relatively unknown activity. It can be thought of as geocaching without the handheld technology. More specifically, it involves an outdoor scavenger hunt organized similarly to geocaching in that it often uses a website to share information. In contrast to geocaching, however, technology is not used to provide explicit directions to letterboxes or to navigate to them. Instead, participants search by following clues (available on the website or, in some cases, passed around by word of mouth), which often refer to natural features. In this way, letterboxing offers a distinct advantage over orienteering and geocaching because it requires students to focus on their environment rather than looking down at a compass, GPS unit, or smartphone.

Two main websites are used for letterboxing: www.letterboxing.org and www.atlasquest.com. Both offer useful content explaining the basics of letterboxing and how to get started. As with geocaching, we recommend introducing your students to the activity via these websites before having them participate in the activity.

Also, as with geocaching, you must identify an outdoor location close to the school for the setting of this activity. Here again, city, state, and regional parks are popular locations for letterboxing, and several letterboxes may be placed at such sites within a 1-mile (1.6-km) radius. This concentration allows students to hunt for more than one box in a relatively short time. Otherwise, you can construct your own letterboxing course on school grounds or at a nearby park. If you construct your own course, place inspirational sayings in the boxes.

At the chosen location, divide each team into two groups. Allow students to find as many boxes containing inspirational sayings as they can in the time available. Some letterbox destinations consist of single boxes, whereas others consist of a series of boxes connected with each other—clues for subsequent boxes will be in the previous boxes. Here is a sample letterboxing clue that could be used on school grounds: "Your goal is to run fast in order to collect your inspirational saying and your next clue. You will get a real kick out of the inspirational saying that you find." Meaning: The letterbox is located behind the soccer goal.

Rules

1. Ensure that students leave letterboxes and inspirational sayings exactly as they were found.

2. Students stay together in their respective groups at all times; they work together to find boxes.

3. Take extra safety precautions since students will be out of your sight while searching for boxes. Each group should have a working cell phone with which to contact you in case of emergency.

4. In case of an injury, one student should stay with the injured student while the others leave to find you and lead you to the injured student.

Variations

- Instead of having students search for boxes with clues obtained from a website, create your own letterboxing course at a location convenient for your class. The boxes and clues do not have to be shared via a website but can simply be shared in writing by your students.

- Letterboxing provides limitless possibilities for adaptation to educational goals for any age. For example, boxes can contain questions for students to discuss among themselves before moving to the next box. They can also contain math problems, word scrambles, or other activities connected to the curriculum.

- Students can create their own letterboxing courses and share them directly with their classmates or post them to a letterboxing website.

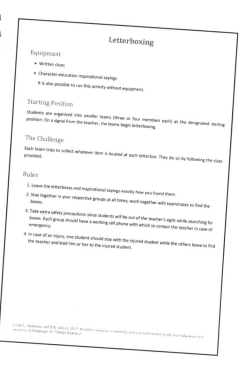

Character Connection Challenge

Equipment

- Whatever nature provides for students to build with
- Bag containing 10 character-education focus words

Description

Each team selects one person to draw a character-education focus word from the bag. After all teams have drawn a word, the members of each team must spell their word using their bodies and items from nature—for example, grass, leaves, sticks, rocks, hay, or sand. One team member, chosen by the team, serves as the builder and directs or assists the team in creating the word. The builder is the only team member who may speak during the activity. The builder is not part of the team's word but notifies you when the word has been completed. You should not know in advance what word the team is spelling; this lack of knowledge enables you to determine whether the team's rendition of the word is really readable. If you cannot understand it, walk away and come back in five minutes. This interval gives the team another chance to make its word legible.

Rules

1. Only the builder may speak.
2. Each team must collect at least 10 items from nature to use in constructing its word.
3. When constructing the word with their bodies and the collected items from nature, the builder may not touch any teammate.
4. The builder calls the teacher over when the team is ready; if the teacher understands the word, then the team has successfully completed the challenge.
5. If any rule is broken, the group must sit and wait for two minutes before starting construction again.

Variations

- Specify how many team members may lie down, sit, or stand. For instance, specify that only five team members may be lying down when the word is finished; the rest of the team must be sitting, standing, or kneeling.
- Start with shorter character words (e.g., caring, honest, pride), then move to longer words (e.g., perseverance, diligence).
- Require each team to make the word using at least three items from nature.
- Allow each team to use any items (e.g., bike, playground log) in constructing its word.
- Allow all team members to speak.
- Time the activity to see how long it takes to construct a legible word. Which team was the fastest?
- Take a picture of each word rendering and post the pictures in the gym.

Character Connection Challenge

Equipment

- Whatever nature provides for the team to build with
- Character-education focus word obtained from the teacher

Starting Position

Each team is grouped together, waiting to select a word from the teacher.

The Challenge

After a team has selected its word, the team members select the items from nature (e.g., grass, leaves, sticks, rocks, hay, sand) that they will use in making the word. One team member, chosen by the team, serves as the builder and directs or assists the other team members in creating the word. Only the builder may speak. The builder is not part of the word but does notify the teacher when the word is completed.

Rules

- One team member should be selected by the team to draw the word out of the bag. The team should all agree as to who is selected.
- Only the builder may speak; all other team members must remain silent while building the word.
- A team's word may not be built using only the team members' bodies; it must also contain at least two different items from nature.
- The builder may not touch any teammate.
- The builder calls the teacher over when the word is done. If the teacher understands the word, then the team has completed the challenge. If not, the group can try to make it more readable, but the teacher will not return to the group until five minutes have passed.
- If any rule is broken, the group must sit and wait for five minutes before starting construction again.

Completion of the Task

The task is complete when the constructed word incorporates all team members and at least two items from nature *and* the teacher can read it.

From L. Anderson and D.R. Glover, 2017, *Building character, community, and a growth mindset in physical education web resource* (Champaign, IL: Human Kinetics).

Group Construction

This activity can be quite difficult for younger students. See the Variations section for possible modifications.

Equipment

Three sets of four items each (or four sets of three items each) from nature (e.g., sticks, rocks, leaves, grass, branches, berries)—enough for each team member to have an identical set of 12 items

Description

The members of each team sit in a semicircle with their backs to the center of the circle. They should not be able to see other group members' equipment as they each build their own design on the ground.

One team member is designated as the construction manager and sits with his or her back to the rest of the team. The team will sit in a semicircle, and the construction manager will sit in front of the semicircle with his or her back to the team. The construction manager places his or her natural objects on the ground one at a time in order to build a design of his or her choosing. After placing each item on the ground, the manager speaks to the rest of the team (without turning around to face them) in order to guide them in placing the same item in the same position. In this way, the manager tries to get all teammates to construct the same design that he or she is building.

Rules

1. Only the construction manager may speak.
2. The construction manager must give directions one item at a time.
3. No one may look at the construction manager's design or at any other builder's design before completion.

4. The construction manager may not look at the other builders' designs before completion. After the construction manager gives the direction for the last item, the builders and the construction manager look at each other's designs. How many designs exactly matched the construction manager's design?

5. After one person has had a chance to be the construction manager, allow another student to attempt that challenge.

Variations

- Allow the builders to ask questions of the construction manager.
- Let one student observe the builders and the construction manager's directions and give feedback to the builders based on his or her vision of the design.
- Let the builders work together as one team.
- Add more construction items.

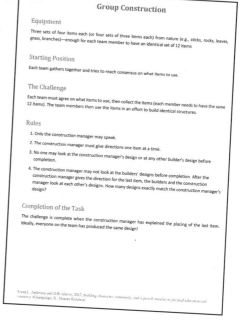

Group Construction

Equipment

Three sets of four items each (or four sets of three items each) from nature (e.g., sticks, rocks, leaves, grass, branches)—enough for each team member to have an identical set of 12 items

Starting Position

Each team gathers together and tries to reach consensus on what items to use.

The Challenge

Each team must agree on what items to use, then collect the items (each member needs to have the same 12 items). The team members then use the items in an effort to build identical structures.

Rules

1. Only the construction manager may speak.
2. The construction manager must give directions one item at a time.
3. No one may look at the construction manager's design or at any other builder's design before completion.
4. The construction manager may not look at the builders' designs before completion. After the construction manager gives the direction for the last item, the builders and the construction manager look at each other's designs. How many designs exactly match the construction manager's design?

Completion of the Task

The challenge is complete when the construction manager has explained the placing of the last item. Ideally, everyone on the team has produced the same design!

From L. Anderson and D.R. Glover, 2017, *Building character, community, and a growth mindset in physical education* (Champaign, IL: Human Kinetics).

Team-Building Race

Equipment

- One item for each student (e.g., football, soccer ball, flying disc)—not necessarily the same item for everyone
- One container per team to hold the team's items (about the same size for all teams)
- One cone per team to designate the starting point

Description

Divide each team into two smaller teams so that you have 8 to 10 teams, each consisting of about four members. This activity can be considered competitive, so have each team do a team break and cheer before starting, and when the activity is over, they should exchange high fives.

Place the boxes at one end of the activity area, at least 50 yards (45 m) away and positioned directly opposite their respective teams, who are sitting with their items by their cones at the other end of the gym or field. On your signal, each team works to get all of its items into its box *five times* as quickly as possible (the activity is timed). Each time a team gets all of its items into its box, the team members exchange high fives and yell "done!" Then, working as a team, they remove the items from their box and run back around to their starting cone. Now they transport the items to the box in a different manner. This process continues until they have completed it five times. When the team yells "done!" for the fifth time, inform the team members of their time.

Revisit this challenge during the next class meeting and have each team try to beat its previous time. Then add the times for the two smaller groups from each larger team and give each larger team its total time. Make sure that all teams exchange high fives and congratulate the other teams. At the next class meeting, each team can try again for a new best time, or you can approach it as a competitive activity among teams.

Rules

1. The team must get all of its items into its container in five different ways. For example, if team members run to the container from the starting cone while carrying the equipment in one round, they may not use that method again.

2. Once a given piece of equipment is used in one round, it may be used in another round *only* if it is transported differently (thus counting as a different method).

3. When the team retrieves equipment from the container, one team member may not retrieve it all; rather, all team members must each carry an item back to the starting cone.

Team-Building Race

Equipment

- One item for each student (e.g., football, soccer ball, flying disc)—not necessarily the same item for everyone
- One container per team to hold the team's items (about the same size for all teams)
- One cone per team to designate the starting point

Starting Position

Each team is divided into two smaller teams so that there are 8 to 10 teams. Each team gathers around its cone and prepares to transport its items to its container, which is located at the other end of the activity area.

The Challenge

On a signal from the teacher, each team works to get all of its items into its box *five times* as quickly as possible.

Rules

1. The team must get all of its items into its container in five different ways. For example, if, in the first round, the team members run to the container from the starting cone while carrying the equipment, they may not use that method again.

2. Once a given piece of equipment is used in one round, it may be used in another round *only* if it is transported differently (thus counting as a different method).

3. When the team retrieves the equipment from the container, one member may not retrieve it all; rather, all team members must each bring an item back to the starting cone.

From L. Anderson and D.R. Glover, 2017, *Building character, community, and a growth mindset in physical education web resource* (Champaign, IL: Human Kinetics).

Variations

- Use different pieces of equipment; be creative and make it challenging!
- Make it a team race to see which team completes the task first.
- See if a team can break its own record during another attempt.
- At least one method must involve tossing or throwing the items to teammates.

Orienteering

Adapted, by permission, from Paul Shirilla.

Equipment

- One compass for every group of students (two, three, or four members each)
- One copy per group of the Orienteering Short Course form (provided in the web resource)
- Three index cards per group, each bearing a character-education focus word (e.g., discipline, enthusiasm, motivation, generosity, confidence, initiative, resilience, respectfulness, loyalty, courage)
- Pencil for each group

Orienteering Short Course Form

Starting location: _____

On a bearing of _____, walk _____ paces.

On a bearing of _____, walk _____ paces.

On a bearing of _____, walk _____ paces.

From L. Anderson and D.R. Glover, 2017, *Building character, community, and a growth mindset in physical education web resource* (Champaign, IL: Human Kinetics)

Description

This activity introduces students to orienteering—specifically, how to shoot and follow a bearing and how to create and follow a short orienteering course. The activity can be done in any relatively open outdoor area.

Divide each team into two groups (two, three, or four members each) and provide each group with a compass, a copy of the Orienteering Short Course form, and at least three index cards each bearing a character-education focus word.

Show students how to shoot a bearing with a compass.

1. Hold the compass flat with the direction-of-travel arrow facing away from you.
2. While keeping the compass flat, raise it to eye level and align the direction-of-travel arrow with the object or landmark for which you want to provide a bearing from your current location.
3. Turn the housing dial until the magnetic arrow (usually red) rests inside of the orienting arrow (usually red with V-shaped lines through its body). Here is a common phrase for describing this process: "Put Red (i.e., the magnetic arrow) in the Shed (i.e., the orienting arrow)."
4. Read the bearing that aligns with the direction-of-travel arrow (also called the index line) at the top of the compass.

Now, show students how to follow a bearing with a compass.

1. Hold the compass flat with the direction-of-travel arrow facing away from you.
2. Provide a sample bearing (e.g., 242 degrees). Turn the housing until the base of the direction-of-travel arrow (i.e., index line) at the top of the dial matches the sample bearing number.
3. Touch the back edge of the compass to your belly button. Turn your body until the magnetic arrow rests inside the orienting arrow (i.e., "Put Red in the Shed").
4. Follow the direction-of-travel arrow for the appropriate number of paces to reach the designated landmark.

Once students have become competent in both shooting and following a bearing, allow each group to construct its own short course, such as, "On a bearing of 242 degrees, walk 100 paces. Now give the compass to another team member and walk 50 paces on a bearing of 320 degrees. Give the compass to a third team member and walk 25 paces on a bearing of 20 degrees." Each group begins by choosing a starting point for its course and noting it on the Orienteering Short Course form (available in the web resource). The group then shoots its first bearing to a landmark, counts the paces required to reach it, and notes the bearing and number of paces on the form. The group places a character-education card somewhere on the landmark. Next, the group shoots another bearing to a different landmark, documents the bearing and the required paces on the form, and places a card on this landmark. The group repeats this process a final time for the third landmark.

Once the course is complete, the group returns to the central area (where you remain while the groups work). Once all groups have returned to you, they swap forms, and each group works to follow the directions provided by another group. Each time a group reaches a landmark, its members remove the card and note the find on their form. Once the group collects all three cards in the course, its members return to the central location.

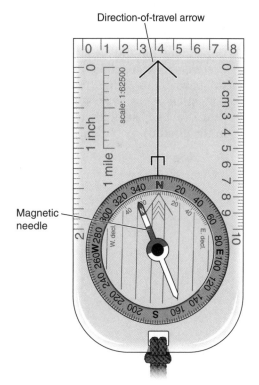

Direction-of-travel arrow

Magnetic needle

Rules

1. To make the courses manageable, the distance to a landmark should be no more than 150 paces.

2. In each group, members serve in the roles of compass manager, pace manager, and scribe. They rotate responsibilities after reaching each landmark so that each student practices all responsibilities. If a group has more than three team members, each team member may not rotate enough to assume all responsibilities but will get a good idea of the responsibilities by participating in the challenge—in both the construction and the following of each course.

3. Before leaving the area, account for all items used; this should be accomplished automatically if all groups successfully follow the courses indicated. However, if a group is unable to find a certain landmark, it may need help from the group that created the course.

Variation

Depending on the weather and your preference, you might allow students to leave items other than character-education focus words (e.g., inspirational sayings, stickers, toothpick flags in the ground).

Orienteering

Equipment

- One compass for each group of students (two, three, or four members each)
- One copy per group of the Orienteering Short Course form
- Three index cards per group, each bearing a character-education focus word
- Writing implement for each group

Starting Position

Students are gathered in groups of two to four, and some members are assigned to the specific roles of compass manager, pace manager, and scribe. Students are ready to plan and construct a short orienteering course.

The Challenge

Once the students have developed compass skills, each team plans and builds a short orienteering course and plots its course on the Orienteering Short Course form. Once the course is complete, the group returns to the central area. After all of the groups have returned, have the groups swap forms. Every group works to follow the course directions it received during the swap. Each time a group reaches a landmark, its members remove the card and note the find on the form. Once a group collects all three cards in the course, its members return to the central location.

Rules

1. To make the courses manageable, the distance to each landmark should be no more than 150 paces.

2. Group members are assigned to fill the roles of compass manager, pace manager, and scribe. Students rotate responsibilities after reaching each landmark so that each student has a chance to become familiar with all responsibilities. In a four person group, the students may not get to all of the responsibilities in both the construction and the following of a course.

3. Before leaving the area, account for all items used; this should be accomplished automatically if all groups successfully follow the courses indicated. However, if a group is unable to find a certain landmark, it may need help from the group that created the course.

From L. Anderson and D.R. Glover, 2017, *Building character, community, and a growth mindset in physical education* (Champaign, IL: Human Kinetics).

Positive Adjectives

Equipment

Positive adjective cards

Description

We have been using positive adjectives for a long time. However, we did not use this activity when we first started to do team building, as we did not want to take the time away from doing the challenges. But after trying positive adjectives several times, we quickly discovered its value and now use it regularly. Positive adjectives should be done at the end of the team-building unit. To set up for this activity, each team is configured in a semicircle with one teammate sitting in the middle and facing his or her teammates. Each team member has a list of the positive adjectives, which can be found in the chapter 2 web resource.

To perform the activity, the team members in the semicircle each take a turn selecting three of the adjectives on the sheet that describe the person sitting in the middle and stating their choices. The students can use only the terms listed on the sheet, and they are not allowed to embellish. The statements should sound something like this: "Mike, you are strong, daring, and humorous." Making such statements is initially difficult for many students, but they usually begin looking forward to it by the next team-building unit. When everyone has had a turn, the students rotate positions so that a new team member goes to the center. Encourage each student to say thank you upon hearing each positive statement.

Positive Adjectives		
Kind	Neat	Strong
Nice	Happy	Active
Cheerful	Courteous	Honest
Clever	Inventive	Imaginative
Enthusiastic	Helpful	Patient
Bright	Thoughtful	Determined
Convincing	Wise	Creative
Independent	Humorous	Pleasant
Delightful	Calm	Confident
Friendly	Inclusive	Empathic
Tolerant	Funny	Caring
Compassionate	Generous	Outgoing

From T. Anderson and D.R. Glover 2017, *Building character, community, and a growth mindset in physical education* (Champaign, IL: Human Kinetics).

Variation

Have each person pick one or two positive adjectives *and* provide a specific reason for each choice. Here are two examples: "Janai, you are friendly—you always let me go first." "Janai, you are creative—you come up with good ideas."

SUMMARY

It can be challenging to teach team building, but don't give up! One physical education teacher was heard saying, "I tried team building with my class, and it was a disaster!" He went on to say that the students had argued the whole time and that he would never do it again. What he—like many teachers and coaches—didn't realize is that this is the beauty of it! You are teaching young people that there is another way. Without this education, many students are left with their go-to behaviors for addressing frustration and failure—namely, arguing, complaining, and giving up. But when you help them develop a growth mindset, they learn how to embrace the obstacles that one inevitably encounters in pursuit of success. If, on the other hand, a teacher or coach allows students and athletes to try team-building challenges without first teaching them how to encourage each other and overcome adversity, then the effort may indeed result in disaster.

When team-building activities are handled effectively, however, students and athletes gain long-lasting memories thanks to the emotions elicited by working through physical challenges. They remember, for example, the feeling of significance and acceptance that comes from belonging to a team, the pride and confidence that result from persevering through adversity, and the joy and enthusiasm associated with taking risks and eventually succeeding. More importantly, the teamwork skills that your students and athletes develop through physical team-building challenges will benefit them for the rest of their lives, both personally and professionally. Team building through physical challenges is also one of the best ways to teach teamwork and how to work positively through failure and frustration. Experiencing both failure and success in a supportive, controlled environment teaches students a growth mindset at its best.

Teamwork, problem solving, a growth mindset, and collaboration are some of the most highly sought-after skills in the workplace. If you want to maximize both growth and performance in youth, you *must* help them understand the value of working together and overcoming adversity.

Facilitating a Growth Mindset Through Reflection, Goal Setting, and Assessment

Setting a goal is not the main thing. It is deciding how you will go about achieving it and then staying with the plan.

Tom Landry, NFL football coach legend

Reaching a goal typically comes at an expense. We often have to make sacrifices; we also make mistakes, and obstacles get in the way. However, we can anticipate and embrace these challenges if we develop a growth mindset. This chapter takes a deeper look at how to facilitate a growth mindset through reflection, assessment, and goal setting.

Individuals who maintain a growth mindset understand that hard work and adversity are essential to growth and learning. In contrast, people with a fixed mindset believe that one's talents and abilities are static: If you can't do it now, you will never be able to do it. As a result, they often give up easily and avoid taking risks.

179

Therefore, if we want our students and athletes to reach their full potential, we must help them develop a growth mindset. In order to cultivate a growth mindset, we need to understand the importance of reflection and goal setting. Learning from past mistakes and building on strengths and weaknesses allow us to strive for continuous improvement. We learn how to constructively work through roadblocks and gain confidence in the process of doing so. Instead of telling ourselves, "I can't do it," our mindset shifts to, "I can't do it yet." We need to facilitate this understanding by modeling it in our own actions.

GROWTH MINDSET AND REFLECTION

Reflection is the link between goal setting and assessment; in fact, it plays a key role both in improving and in reaching goals. Even so, it is underappreciated and underused. We learn by doing, but we learn even more by doing *and* reflecting. Our experiences, successes, trials, and errors are our best teachers—if we take the time to reflect and learn from them. Consider, for example, the use of game film and other kinds of video documentation of performance. Many of the most successful athletes in the world note that video of themselves in action gives them a powerful tool for improvement. It enables them to take a step back, analyze what is going well and not so well, and make necessary changes. This is what being a reflective learner is all about!

At the same time, humans are, by nature, forward thinkers. We tend to think about what's next, what new content or skills need to be introduced so that our students or athletes continue to learn and improve. The mentality goes something like this: "The more we do, the more we practice, the more we are exposed to—the faster we learn and grow." It is through reflection, however, that our students and athletes can be most successful and their growth and learning most meaningful. Reflection also encourages students to invest in the process of their own learning because it actively involves them in their journey toward achievement and success.

Before expecting students to become reflective learners, however, we must teach them how to do so. At first, students often struggle with reflection because they have rarely been given the opportunity to engage in it. Instead, they are typically *told* what they are doing right or wrong and what they need to do in order to improve. If, instead, we help them develop a daily or weekly habit of reflection, they quickly gain the skills and appreciate the opportunity. Here are a few general reflection questions that can be integrated easily into most any situation:

- What could I have done differently?
- What improvements can I make?
- What resources did I use to help me when things got difficult?
- What is it that I am most proud of and would like to share with others?

When students and athletes develop a growth mindset, they improve more quickly and become much more motivated to reach their goals. They also recognize that the obstacles standing in their way are really only opportunities to learn and grow stronger. As a result, they seek out the resources needed to overcome challenges and solve problems. The way to help your students develop these skills is to facilitate their understanding of a growth mindset through reflection.

Self-Assessment

The web resource for this chapter includes a self-assessment to help students and athletes reflect on whether they have more of a fixed mindset or a growth mindset. Before asking students to reflect, make sure that they understand that learning and growth are reinforced and strengthened when they take time to learn from their actions. Student's initial responses to this form may be used to establish a baseline before you provide formal instruction regarding a growth mindset and a fixed mindset. Having students complete the form at the beginning of the year or season and again at the end is an excellent way to track growth.

The term *reflection* is sometimes used interchangeably with *metacognition*, which means being aware and in control of one's own thought processes (Fraser-Thill, 2016). Research shows that developing strong metacognitive skills is one of the most effective ways to increase both achievement and motivation. In addition, students who have developed metacognitive skills are more likely to develop a growth mindset, as well as greater resilience. One form of metacognition involves thinking about why we make certain choices and what we might do differently.

Self-Assessment: Growth Mindset Versus Fixed Mindset

For each of the following items, rate yourself on a scale of 1 to 10, with 10 being the highest. To indicate your rating, put an X on the number line in the appropriate place.

Learning Logs

Learning logs are referred to by a number of names, including growth logs, goal trackers, and reflective journals. By any name, the point of such logs is to track one's growth and to create opportunities for reflection. Prompting students to engage in reflective activities is a great way to track growth and reinforce a growth mindset.

The first few times that students are asked to reflect by completing a log or flow chart they are likely to write very little. The reason is that such reflection does not necessarily come naturally. As with many other things, students need to practice reflection in order to get better at it. Fortunately, by making time each week for students to reflect, and consistently using the same routine, you help them become more comfortable with reflection, and a growth mindset starts to feel more natural. As students begin to understand the benefits of the process, they will be more open with their thoughts. As always, reinforce the positive by sharing well-done student examples with the rest of the class; of course this should be done only with the student's permission, and it can remain anonymous.

To help students recognize their growth, have them keep a "growth binder" or "growth folder" containing all of their reflections in order by date. The binder also gives you a great tool for use in conferencing, both with parents and with your students or athletes. Reflection and a growth mindset are connected in the example provided in figure 6.1.

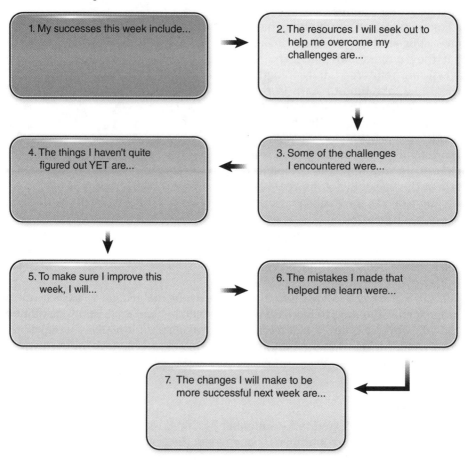

Weekly Reflection

Week of:

How successful were you this week? What have you learned and what will you do differently to ensure continued growth next week?

1. My successes this week include...

2. The resources I will seek out to help me overcome my challenges are...

3. Some of the challenges I encountered were...

4. The things I haven't quite figured out YET are...

5. To make sure I improve this week, I will...

6. The mistakes I made that helped me learn were...

7. The changes I will make to be more successful next week are...

FIGURE 6.1 Sample weekly reflection.

GROWTH MINDSET AND SELF-ASSESSMENT

Assessment is a form of reflection, and it's typically done by the teacher or coach. When engaging in self-assessment, students use higher-order thinking skills, which are often referred to collectively as critical thinking. When students think critically, their motivation and learning increase. They are empowered when they become actively involved in their learning and feel a sense of control in the decision-making process. It is much more fun to think, evaluate, and make choices than to merely memorize things!

Too often, assessment is used merely as a means to give a grade or evaluate learning. However, assessment geared toward motivating and reinforcing learning is much more effective than mere assessment of learning. When teachers do the thinking and analyzing, they are also doing the learning. Instead, we need to give ownership to students so that *they* do the thinking, analyzing, and therefore, the learning. In order to maximize the benefits of self-assessment, we need to continually nurture and reinforce a growth mindset. When students understand that everyone can learn and improve, they are more likely to be honest in their self-assessments and increasingly open to constructive feedback from others. Two types of self-assessment are determining a baseline and engaging in end-of-unit (or end-of-season) self-assessment.

Determining a Baseline

We can use baseline data gathered through self-assessment to determine what a student or athlete knows before the unit or season begins. In addition, if we compare that data with the results of an identical or similar self-assessment at the end of the unit, we can track growth. Figure 6.2 shows a baseline assessment for basketball that can be modified for other specific units and for various participant ages.

FIGURE 6.2

Sample Baseline Self-Assessment for Basketball

- What are the three most important concepts to being a successful basketball *player*?
- What are the three most important concepts to being a successful basketball *team*?
- In what areas of the game do you hope to improve?
- What are your strengths as a basketball player?
- On a scale of 1 to 10, with 10 being the highest, rate your *basketball* skill level:

  Score: _____

  Explain your score:
- On a scale of 1 to 10, with 10 being the highest, rate your *teamwork* skill level:

  Score: _____

  Explain your score:
- What are your goals for this unit? (List at least two.)

  At the end of this unit, I hope to _____.
- What do you need to do in order to reach your goals?
- What resources will you seek out when you have questions or face obstacles?

End-of-Unit Evaluation

The end-of-unit (or end-of-season) evaluation uses many of the same reflection questions as the baseline evaluation, but students are likely to answer them differently because of what they have learned throughout the unit. Once students complete their end-of-unit self-assessments, allow each student to compare the results with those from the beginning-of-year assessment. This comparison also provides great data for you as teacher or coach. For an example, see figure 6.3.

During the unit or season, students should engage in a weekly learning reflection (see figure 6.1). When students consistently practice reflection and continually integrate language that is connected to a growth mindset, they become more motivated and make more progress. Here are some reflection questions that can be used weekly with any unit or sport:

- What went well that I can build on?
- What could I improve?
- What do I need to do in order to improve?
- What would I change?
- Have I tried my best?
- Do I seek resources when I have questions or face obstacles?

GROWTH MINDSET AND GOAL SETTING

Goal setting is another motivating technique that—if done effectively—can help students and athletes maximize their performance. Goal setting is a meaningful activity when the individual follows through on goals and regularly reflects on progress. All too often, however, after goals are set, they are left alone. When teachers and coaches ask students and athletes to set goals, they often have the best intentions. Then, however, the "full speed ahead" mentality kicks in, and we often fail to recognize or prioritize the power of slowing down and going deeper.

Success breeds motivation. When students and athletes are given the opportunity to track their growth and celebrate their successes along the way, they are intrinsically motivated to continue striving for improvement. When they also develop a growth mindset, learn to expect setbacks, and develop skills to persevere through those setbacks, they are less likely to give up.

The most popular format for goal setting is the SMART process; there is no question that using this model is an effective way to set goals. However, for students to learn how to reach their goals, we need to emphasize not only goal setting but also goal *getting*. To that end, we introduce here a goal-getting format that aligns with a growth mindset. This new format, referred to as GROWTH (see sidebar), addresses the obstacles that are inevitably encountered in pursuing a goal and presents a plan for tracking progress.

FIGURE 6.3

End-of-Unit (or End-of-Season) Self-Assessment for Basketball

- What are the three most important concepts to being a successful basketball *player*?
- What are the three most important concepts to being a successful basketball *team*?
- In what areas of the game do to you hope to improve?
- What are your strengths as a basketball player?
- What are three things that you learned during this unit?
- In what areas did you improve the most?
- On a scale of 1 to 10, with 10 being the highest, rate your *basketball* skill level:

  Score: _____

  Explain your score:

- On a scale of 1 to 10, with 10 being the highest, rate your *teamwork* skill level:

  Score: _____

  Explain your score:

- On a scale of 1 to 10, with 10 being the highest, rate your *effort* during this unit or season:

  Score: _____

  Explain your score:

- Did you reach the goals that you set for yourself at the beginning of the unit or season? Why or why not?
- What resources did you seek out when you had questions or faced obstacles?
- From the beginning of the unit or season to the end, how have your feelings or attitudes toward basketball changed as a result of your experience?

GROWTH

G: Goal

What specific goal do I want to accomplish and by what date? (Include baseline information.)

Example: By March, 1, 2017, I want to exercise at least 240 minutes per week (specific goal), which translates to about 34 minutes per day. Currently, I exercise only about 30 minutes every other day, which totals to about 105 minutes per week (baseline).

R: Realistic Plan

What specific actions will I take to reach my goal? When, where, what, and how often?

Example: On four out of five days during the work week, I will go for a brisk 40-minute walk when I get home from work. If it rains, I will do yoga in the house. On the weekend, I will go for a 60-minute combination walk/run at the nature center.

O: Obstacles

What obstacles might I encounter as I strive to reach my goal? How will I turn those obstacles into opportunities?

Examples

- If I'm tired, I may just want to sit and watch TV before dinner. I will always try to make arrangements with a walking partner on the day before; that way, it won't be as easy to skip walking.
- My knee may start bothering me with the increased walking and running. If my knee starts bothering me, I will do yoga every other day and bike instead of walking. I will also look for other ways to exercise.
- I may get busy and feel like I don't have time to exercise. If I know I am going to have a busy day, I will set my alarm 30 minutes early and walk before work.

W: Who and What?

Who will I look to when I encounter obstacles or get stuck? What resources will I seek out for help?

Examples

- I will make arrangements with Joni, Mark, or Fatimah to exercise. I will plan to exercise with each person on the same day each week.
- I will share my goal with each person and show him or her my plan. I will ask them to ask me how my goal is going and hold me accountable for meeting on our scheduled date.
- If my knee starts bothering me, I will seek out physical therapy exercises to help. I will also check with the local fitness club, Fitness Focus, to learn about other exercises I can do that won't bother my knee.

T: Tracking

How will I track my growth? What tools will I use to monitor progress (e.g., journal, growth log)? How often will I track my progress and engage in reflection?

Example: I will purchase a daily calendar and record the number of minutes that I exercise each day. I will add up the total minutes for the week on Sunday and try to increase my time by five minutes each week until I reach 240 minutes per week for three weeks in a row.

H: Habits

What new habits do I need to create in order to reach my goal? Once I reach my goal, what habits will I need to maintain in order to sustain my growth?

Examples

- My new daily routine has become habitual. I want to keep the same schedule. I need to make sure that I exercise in the morning on Saturday or Sunday, because if I don't, it can be tough to find time during the day.

- I want to continue to track the number of minutes that I exercise each week. It's very motivating to add up the minutes every Sunday. I find that I want to exercise more each week.

- I will keep the same walking buddies. They have been very supportive, and I really enjoy their company!

Reinforce the importance of making time for weekly reflection. The more that students and athletes engage in reflection, the more habitual it becomes. Weekly practice is not only a great way to teach reflection; it is also an excellent monitoring guide to help track progress made toward goals. A sample weekly self-assessment form (GROWTH Self-Assessment for Goal Getting) is provided in the web resource.

SUMMARY

If you want to maximize your students' or athletes' performance, you must first facilitate their understanding of a growth mindset, then provide them with opportunities to practice and reinforce it through reflection, self-assessment, and goal getting. Of course, teachers and coaches need to help students and

GROWTH Self-Assessment for Goal Getting

Date:	Attempting (beginning)	Almost there (continued effort needed)	Yes! I'm where I need to be to reach my goal.	I'm doing better than I thought! I've exceeded my own expectations.
G: Goal How is my overall progress toward reaching my goal?				
R: Realistic Plan Do my choices support the plan I have in place?				
O: Obstacles Am I learning as a result of the obstacles I encounter?				
W: Who and What? Have I determined at least three people or resources I can turn to when setbacks occur?				
T: Tracking Am I tracking my growth in a journal to measure it?				
H: Habits What new habits am I forming that contribute to my success?				
What is going well that I need to continue? What changes need to be made in order to reach my goal?				

From J. Anderson and D.R. Glover, 2017, *Building character, community, and a growth mindset in physical education with the power of the Connecticut, IL: Human Kinetics).*

athletes know what to learn; just as important, however, we need to teach them *how* to learn. Individuals feel empowered when they are equipped with the skills necessary to reach goals and overcome adversity. In addition, when students are actively involved in shaping their own journey toward growth, their motivation increases and their growth is expedited.

Learning and growing are processes that often involve both joy and discomfort. Understanding this reality through the lens of a growth mindset is one of the best gifts that you can give your students or athletes. Not only will you notice great improvement in student growth, but also you are preparing your students and athletes to effectively navigate the trials and tribulations they will encounter in life.

REFERENCES

Fraser-Thill, R. (2016). What is the definition of metacognition? Retrieved from https://www.verywell.com/what-is-metacognition-3288021.

About the Authors

Leigh Anderson currently teaches in White Bear Lake, Minnesota, where she applies many of the concepts in this book. In addition to her elementary classroom and intervention experience, Leigh taught at the graduate level in the masters of teaching and learning program at Saint Mary's University of Minnesota. This is the second book that Leigh has coauthored dealing with best practices in education, and she has presented both nationally and internationally. Leigh holds a bachelor's degree in elementary education and a master's degree in curriculum and instruction.

Courtesy of Leigh Anderson

Donald R. Glover has taught physical education, including adapted physical education, since 1967 at the preschool, elementary, secondary, and postsecondary levels. He currently teaches elementary physical education methods at the University of Wisconsin at River Falls.

In 1981, Glover was recognized as Minnesota's Teacher of the Year, and he was named the Minnesota Adapted Physical Education Teacher of the Year in 1989. He has written seven books, published numerous magazine and journal articles on physical education and sport, and been a clinician at more than 100 workshops and clinics.

Glover earned his master's degree in physical education from Winona State University in 1970. A former president of the Minnesota Association for Health, Physical Education, Recreation and Dance, he is a member of SHAPE America, the National Association of Sport and Physical Education (NASPE), and the Minnesota Education Association.

Courtesy of Donald R. Glover